DEMOCRACY
IN THE ISLANDS

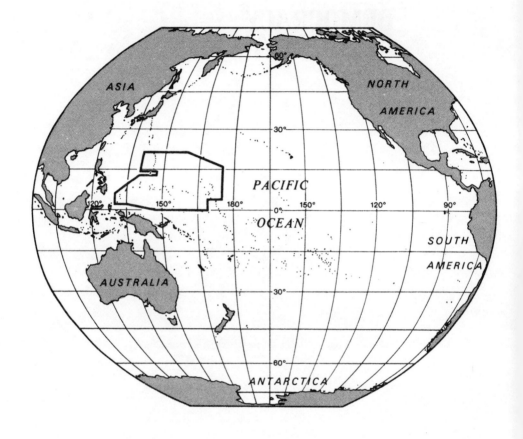

The U.S. Trust Territory of the Pacific Islands, which includes most of
Micronesia, is made up of 2,141 islands, 98 of them inhabited. They cover
a land area of only 1,850 square kilometers but are scattered over 7.8
million square kilometers in the western Pacific Ocean.

DEMOCRACY IN THE ISLANDS
THE MICRONESIAN PLEBISCITES OF 1983

AUSTIN RANNEY AND
HOWARD R. PENNIMAN

American Enterprise Institute for Public Policy Research
Washington, D.C.

Austin Ranney is codirector of AEI's Program in Political and Social Processes, a former president of the American Political Science Association, and editor of *Referendums: A Study in Practice and Theory* and *The Referendum Device*.

Howard R. Penniman is codirector of AEI's Program in Political and Social Processes, general editor of AEI's "At the Polls" studies of elections in democratic countries, and an observer of elections in a number of countries, including Bolivia, South Vietnam, El Salvador, and Zimbabwe.

Library of Congress Cataloging in Publication Data

Ranney, Austin.
  Democracy in the Islands.

  (AEI studies ; 420)
  1. Referendum—Micronesia (Federated States)
2. Plebiscite—Micronesia (Federated States)
3. Micronesia (Federated States)—Politics and government.
4. Referendum—Pacific Islands (Trust Territory)
5. Plebiscite—Pacific Islands (Trust Territory)
6. Pacific Islands (Trust Territory)—Politics and government. I. Penniman, Howard Rae, 1916–   II. Title.
III. Series.
JF493.M534R36 1985   328'.2   85-3895
ISBN 0-8447-3577-9
ISBN 0-8447-3576-0 (pbk.)

AEI Studies 420

ON THE COVER: A Palauan voter deposits his marked ballot in a double-lidded ballot box similar to those used in the FSM and the Marshall Islands. The cover photograph and the other photographs in this book were taken by Howard Penniman and Austin Ranney.

Printed in the United States of America

Contents

The Campaign 87
Election Experience and Rules 94
The Plebiscite Results 97
Fairness of the Plebiscite 103

5 REFERENDUMS IN TRADITIONAL SOCIETIES 105
Standards for Democratic Referendums 105
Evaluation of the 1983 Micronesian Plebiscites 106
Conclusion 115

LIST OF TABLES

LIST OF FIGURES

ILLUSTRATIONS

President's Foreword

The research for this study was funded by the United States Information Agency, and its publication is supported by the Asia Foundation. The book, written by Austin Ranney and Howard R. Penniman, the codirectors of AEI's Program in Political and Social Processes, combines two of the program's longstanding interests: the conduct of competitive elections in Western and third world countries, and the role of referendums in democratic government. Although the three Micronesian polities involved have a combined population of less than 120,000, their problems and their future are of major interest for students of Pacific affairs as well as for people concerned with third-world politics in general. The area is of considerable strategic importance for the United States, its political and economic development has been a major test for American administrators and diplomats, and its future is a matter of concern for both the United Nations and the United States.

To conduct its study of the 1983 Micronesian plebiscites, AEI assembled an international team of scholars drawn from The American University, the University of British Columbia, the University of California, Berkeley, and Georgetown University. The six scholars made a total of seven trips to the area, observed the pre-election voter education programs, political campaigns, and voting, and participated in many discussions with Micronesian government and opposition leaders, election administrators, and journalists. Their report is another instance of AEI's continuing concern with democratic institutions and practices as well as with U.S. foreign and defense policies. We believe it sheds useful light on an important, though little known, part of the world.

WILLIAM J. BAROODY, JR.
President
American Enterprise Institute

Foreword

Where is Micronesia? Most people, hearing of the plebiscites described and analyzed in this book, start with that question. But it quickly leads to many others, because the events, so well described here, involve many wider issues such as the part the United Nations, and particularly the Trusteeship Council, have played in the ending of colonialism; the difficulties that administering powers have encountered in fulfilling the tasks undertaken in their trusteeship agreements; and the problems that small and scattered islands with minimal natural resources and a growing population face as they seek to take their place in the international political scene.

The Trust Territory of the Pacific Islands, which comprises most but not all of Micronesia, is the last of the eleven Trust Territories that have been administered under the United Nations Trusteeship system. The other ten, administered variously by Australia, Belgium, France, Italy, New Zealand, and the United Kingdom, have all determined their future. Some have opted for independence; others have chosen to combine with neighboring countries or territories. The process has been as varied as one would expect with the differing geography, history, and, above all, human elements involved.

In the Trusteeship Council of the United Nations interest is now therefore centered on the political future of the Trust Territory of the Pacific Islands. The process of constitutional and political development, so well described in this book, had by the end of 1982 reached the point at which three of the four component parts of the Territory were ready to embark on consulting their people on their future political status by means of plebiscites. The fourth, the Northern Mariana Islands, had already chosen in 1975 to become a United States "Commonwealth." The government of the United States of America, as the administering authority, invited the Trusteeship Council to send missions to observe the three plebiscites—an invitation accepted by the council on December 20, 1982. I found myself, as president of the council, with the interesting task of leading two of the three observer missions.

Although the United Nations missions and the academic teams led by Professor Ranney and Professor Penniman, observed the same things, their interests and perspectives were different. The aims of the UN missions were practical and limited: first, to satisfy ourselves that the voting public understood the issues involved and, second, to satisfy ourselves that the plebiscites were fair and were carried out in accordance with the relevant laws and regulations, ensuring, *inter alia*, the secrecy of the vote and the accuracy of the counting. The findings of the UN missions were published in the official records of the Trusteeship Council.[1]

Professor Ranney and Professor Penniman and their colleagues observed the plebiscites from a different angle. As authorities on electoral processes, they saw these plebiscites in a larger context. They were interested in the social and geographical problems involved; for example, the problem of holding a referendum on complicated constitutional issues where culture is based on the spoken rather than the written word and the problem of organizing a plebiscite in a country consisting of islands scattered over a huge area of the Pacific Ocean. Their book examines the plebiscites in historical depth, not just analyzing the immediate political context in which they were held but also drawing conclusions about Western-style referendums in traditional societies. All this makes rewarding reading, not only for the student of political science but also for the practicing politician and diplomat.

Inevitably the paths of the two observing missions, diplomatic and academic, crossed on many occasions. We were able to exchange impressions to our mutual benefit. Reading both the UN reports and this book, I am struck by the general agreement on all matters which both considered. This is not surprising. I am revealing no confidences when I say that the UN mission, composed as it was of diplomats from four countries representing both the Western and the third worlds, reached agreement on their reports very easily. I find it very satisfactory that Professor Ranney and Professor Penniman, with their far greater knowledge and experience of plebiscites, should have reached similar conclusions. They do us, at the UN missions, the compliment of quoting our reports on many occasions. If only we had had the advantage of reading their book before writing our reports we should, I am sure, have used it extensively. But Professor Ranney and Professor Penniman do what the UN reports could not do: they paint in the complicated sociohistorical background. They compare and contrast the plebiscites and place them in a political context of democratic practices, which only scholars such as the authors could undertake. In short, they have written the definitive book on a fascinating page of political history.

J. W. D. MARGETSON
British Embassy, The Hague

Note

1. Report of the UN Visiting Mission to Observe the Plebiscite in Palau, February 1983 (UN Document T/1851, 1983). Report of the UN Visiting Mission to Observe the Plebiscite in the Federated States of Micronesia, June 1983 (UN Document T/1860, 1983). Report of the UN Visiting Mission to Observe the Plebiscite in the Marshall Islands, September 1983 (UN Document T/1865, 1984).

Preface

This book is a study of the plebiscites held in the Micronesian polities of Palau, the Federated States of Micronesia, and the Marshall Islands in 1983 on the Compact of Free Association with the United States of America. The area called "Micronesia" includes a large number of small and thinly populated islands scattered across an area of the Central Pacific bounded by Hawaii, the Philippines, Japan, and New Guinea. Many of the islands were captured from Japan by the United States in World War II, and in 1947 the United Nations placed most of them in a UN "strategic trust territory" to be administered by the United States.

During the course of the U.S. trusteeship, four distinct Micronesian polities have emerged: the Northern Marianas, Palau, the Federated States of Micronesia, and the Marshall Islands. In 1976 the voters of the Northern Marianas voted to become a Commonwealth of the United States (a status similar though not identical to that of Puerto Rico). The other three polities negotiated with the United States a Compact of Free Association, according to which each Micronesian polity would gain control over its domestic and international affairs with the notable exception that the United States would retain control over the defense and international security of each polity and would provide substantial economic aid to each for at least fifteen years after the Compact went into effect.

In 1983, plebiscites[1] were held in Palau (February), the Federated States of Micronesia (June), and the Marshall Islands (September) in which the voters registered their approval or disapproval of the Compact and also indicated their preferences for independence or some other future status if the Compact were disapproved.

These plebiscites are interesting for several reasons. They interest students of international law because they were a major step in establishing a new and unusual form of international status. They interest students of American strategic affairs because they were a necessary step in defining the American status in a part of the world that was the scene of major fighting in World War II and that remains today an area of considerable strategic significance. They interest students of political, social, and economic development in the third world because they came after centuries of foreign rule—first by Spain, then by imperial Germany, then by Japan, and finally, from the mid-1940s to the mid-1980s, in a trusteeship by the United States.

The present writers, however, are concerned mainly with the conduct of elections in democratic polities. We have analyzed both general elections for public offices and referendum elections on specific issues in more than thirty developed Western-style countries,[2] but we have never before had the opportunity to observe elections conducted in conditions as unusual and demanding as those surrounding the 1983 Micronesian plebiscites. It is therefore not surprising that we eagerly seized the opportunity to make this study when it was presented to us.

In the pages to come we will describe the unusual circumstances of the plebiscites in more detail. We will note here, however, that in many ways they resembled those described by J.-H. Hamel, the chief electoral officer of Canada, in his account of elections among the Indians and Eskimos in Canada's Northwest Territories. Elections in both places have had the following characteristics:

- Very small electorates divided into tiny communities separated from one another by vast distances
- Native cultures built mainly on oral rather than written communications
- Many different native languages and cultures
- A severe climate and a subsistence economy[3]

Micronesia's climate is hot and humid rather than subarctic, and its peoples are scattered over vast expanses of ocean rather than tundra; but in most respects Micronesia's electoral problems are similar to those in Canada's Northwest Territories. And the fact that in both areas those problems have been handled quite well is a matter of both interest and encouragement for observers like Hamel and ourselves.

Let us say a word about the circumstances of and the participants in the study reported here. In 1982 the United States Information Agency made a grant to the American Enterprise Institute to study the 1983 plebiscites and to engage in seminars and other discussions with Micronesian political leaders, public officials, and journalists concerning the plebiscites. The present writers served as the project's codirectors, and we assembled an international roster of the following scholars to work with us:

David Butler, Nuffield College, Oxford University
Alan C. Cairns, University of British Columbia

Eugene C. Lee, University of California, Berkeley
Richard G. Smolka, The American University
Raymond E. Wolfinger, University of California, Berkeley
The roster of scholars was divided into teams, and the teams made the following visits to the three polities:

- Republic of Palau
  Howard Penniman and Richard Smolka, October 1–8, 1982
  Howard Penniman and Richard Smolka, November 18–27, 1982
  Alan Cairns, Howard Penniman, and Richard Smolka, February 3–16, 1983
- Federated States of Micronesia
  Eugene Lee and Austin Ranney, to Ponape and Truk, February 14–22, 1983
  Eugene Lee to Yap, Truk, and Ponape; Richard Smolka to Ponape; Raymond Wolfinger to Truk and Ponape; Austin Ranney to Ponape, June 17–25, 1983
- Republic of the Marshall Islands
  Austin Ranney and Raymond Wolfinger, to Majuro and Kwajalein, November 11–21, 1982
  Richard Smolka, to Majuro, August 8–14, 1983
  Howard Penniman and Richard Smolka, to Majuro, September 1–11, 1983
  Austin Ranney and Raymond Wolfinger, to the East-West Center, University of Hawaii, and to Kwajalein, September 1–11, 1983
  David Butler, to Kwajalein and Majuro, September 1–11, 1983

The observers' scholarly inclinations and the terms of the grant led us to focus on the quality of the elections, not on the merits or demerits of the Compact of Free Association. Most observers of most elections probably develop some preference for one side or another, and very likely we were no exception. From the few and fragmentary remarks our scholars made on the subject, however, we seemed to be divided on the question of how we would have voted had we been Micronesians. In any event, like all scholars of elections, we know that properly conducted elections do not guarantee good results, however defined; and how the Micronesians managed their plebiscites and why they voted as they did, not which side had the best cause, were our concerns.

The purpose of this book is to set forth in some detail our observations and conclusions about the conduct and significance of the plebiscites. In writing it we have been greatly assisted by the special help of Alan Cairns for the chapter on Palau, Eugene Lee for the chapter on the Federated States of Micronesia, and Richard Smolka for the chapter on the Marshall Islands. Brother Henry Schwalben-berg, S.J., read the entire manuscript and made many helpful sugges-tions. We are also deeply grateful to E. C. Downs and Donald Hannaford of the Department of the Interior's Office of Territorial and International Affairs, who guided us skillfully through Micro-nesia's physical, cultural, and political geography; and to Dr. Gregory Winn of the United States Information Agency, who administered our grant with energy and attention. Finally, we are grateful to The Asia Foundation and its president, Ambassador F. Haydn Williams, for the grant supporting the book's publication.

It should be noted, however, that, although our colleagues pro-vided many materials and insights, we who wrote this book are solely responsible for its contents.

Austin Ranney and Howard R. Penniman
Washington, D.C.
January 1985

Notes

1. The term *plebiscites* is sometimes considered synonymous with *referen-dums*—that is, elections in which voters vote directly upon questions of public policy rather than indirectly by choosing the public officials who decide the questions: see David Butler and Austin Ranney, eds., *Referendums: A Study in Practice and Theory* (Washington, D.C.: American Enterprise Institute, 1978), chap. 1; and Jean-Marie Denquin, *Référendum et Plébiscite* (Paris: Librairie générale de droit et de jurisprudence, 1976). Here we follow Denquin's us-age, which defines a plebiscite as a particular kind of referendum in which the voters of a jurisdiction vote directly upon its international and legal status—as was the case in the three Micronesian polities in 1983.

2. The American Enterprise Institute's "At the Polls" series, under the general editorship of Howard R. Penniman, has published more than twenty volumes on the conduct of general elections in major democratic countries, including Australia, Canada, France, Greece, Ireland, Israel, Italy, Japan, New Zealand, Spain, Switzerland, the United Kingdom, and Venezuela. In addition, David Butler, Howard R. Penniman, and Austin Ranney edited *Democracy at the Polls* (Washington, D.C.: American Enterprise Institute, 1981), a cross-sectional study of candidate elections in twenty-eight demo-cratic countries. Austin Ranney has edited volumes on the 1980 and 1984 U.S. national elections. AEI has published several volumes on referendums: David Butler and Austin Ranney, *Referendums*; Anthony King, *Britain Says Yes: The 1975 Referendum on the Common Market* (Washington, D.C.: American Enter-prise Institute, 1977); and Austin Ranney, ed., *The Referendum Device* (Wash-ington, D.C.: American Enterprise Institute, 1981).

3. J.-H. Hamel, "Native Participation in Free Elections: The Case of the Northwest Territories (Canada)," *Electoral Studies*, vol. 2 (1983), pp. 149–154.

1
Prelude to the Plebiscites

Geographers generally include in the area of the Pacific Ocean labeled "Micronesia" (meaning "tiny islands") the islands and atoll chains of the Marianas, Palaus, Carolines, Marshalls, and Gilberts. Spread over a large area of the central Pacific, these islands and atolls are bounded by Hawaii on the east, the Philippines on the west, Japan on the north, and New Guinea and the Solomon Islands on the south. The area covers more than 7.8 million square kilometers of ocean and includes more than 2,100 land masses ranging from relatively large and hilly volcanic islands, such as Ponape and Truk, to small and flat coral islands, such as Jaluit and Enewetak. Taken together, these islands have a combined land area of approximately 1,850 square kilometers and only about 100 of the islands are inhabited. The total population of the area is estimated at 133,000, although it is growing at the rate of 3.6 percent per year—one of the highest growth rates in the world and a source of many of Micronesia's problems. As David Butler sums up, Micronesia is "a vast scattering of islands that spreads . . . over an area larger than Europe but with a land mass smaller than Wales and a population smaller than Oxford's."[1]

The subjects of this book are the plebiscites held in three Micronesian polities in 1983: the Republic of Palau on February 10, the Federated States of Micronesia on June 21; and the Republic of the Marshall Islands on September 7. In each plebiscite the ballot posed two basic questions: (1) Do you approve of free association with the United States as set forth in the Compact of Free Association? (2) What political status should be negotiated and mutually agreed between [the polity] and the United States in the event that free association is rejected? In Palau a third question asked whether, under the compact, the United States should be able to store and transship nuclear materials in Palauan territory and waters.

Before we focus on the specifics in each of the three elections, we will briefly sketch the nature of the Micronesian peoples and polities and the issues they faced in 1983.

Some General Characteristics of Micronesia

Economic Dependence. The Micronesian peoples and polities share certain physical, historical, economic, and cultural characteristics that shape their political processes. One of the most important is their continuing economic dependence. At least since the Japanese suzerainty (c. 1914 to 1944) each of the Micronesian polities has imported many more goods from abroad than it has exported. Throughout the American trusteeship (c. 1946 to the present) the continuing balance of payments deficit has been made up by money provided by the United States. U.S. aid has come in many forms: direct block grants to the Micronesian governments; categorical grants for particular social programs such as housing, public health, Medicare and Medicaid, food stamps, Head Start, and education; and capital improvement grants for projects such as roads, airfields, satellite communications, dredging and harbor improvements, shipping, agricultural research, pest control, sanitation, and public works. The importance of this aid to the Micronesians' present way of life is dramatized by the fact that since the mid-1940s the United States has often provided more than 90 percent of all revenues received by the Micronesian governments, and its annual contributions have never fallen below 80 percent; local taxes have provided the rest.[2]

The Micronesian governments, with U.S. assistance, have launched a number of projects to develop such leading local enterprises as the production of copra, fishing and the leasing of fishing rights, canning, forestry, agriculture, and tourism. They have sought investment by foreign investors, not only from the United States but also from other nations, notably Japan.

Most observers believe that, although significant economic progress can be and is being made, it will be decades before any of the Micronesian polities will even approach economic independence. Until then their only alternative to returning to a subsistence economy is the continued infusion of large amounts of economic aid from abroad. As we shall see, the substantial economic aid the United States will provide to the Micronesian governments under the terms of the Compact of Free Association is scheduled to run for fifteen years after the compact goes into effect; yet no one can say with confidence that aid will be unnecessary after that. This issue of dependence was a major

2

factor in the negotiations concerning the compact and in the decisions that Micronesian voters had to make in 1983 about approving it.

The Traditional Social Structure. Each of the Micronesian polities has a Western-style constitutional government with elected legislators and executives, appointed judges and administrators; one-person-one-vote elections; and many opportunities for the free public expression of political preferences in meetings, pamphlets, posters, newspapers, and radio and television broadcasts. Yet underlying and permeating the Western forms of each polity is its traditional hierarchical social structure.

The social structure of the Marshall Islands offers a good illustration. Beyond the immediate family, the basic social unit for every Marshallese is a small group of people occupying an area—a group similar in size and solidarity to a tribe in other societies. At the base of the group are the *dri jerbals*, the workers or ordinary people. They have a common allegiance to a particular *alab*, the chief of the small local unit. A number of *alabs* in an area are loyal to an *iroij*, who is the chief for a larger area. At the top of the hierarchy stands an *iroij laplap*, a chief of chiefs, who is the acknowledged head of many groups and the areas they inhabit.

Traditionally the people in these groups look to their *alabs* and *iroij* for guidance on many matters, including political decisions. Often when the *iroij* is known to favor a particular course of action—for example, approving the Compact of Free Association—most of his followers will vote that way. It is important to understand, however, that although each *iroij* owns the land on which his followers live and although he has the power to banish them from his area, nevertheless his influence seldom rests on coercion or sanctions (except, perhaps, in the Faichuk district of Truk—see chapter 3). Rather it stems from the desire of his people to be aided in making a decision on a complicated question by advice from someone whose wisdom and reliability they have been reared to trust.

The constitutions of all three polities have provisions intended to preserve the traditional social structures and procedures. The Republic of the Marshall Islands has, in addition to its elected *Nitijela* (parliament), a Council of Iroij composed of the twelve acknowledged *iroij* in the republic. The council considers all bills affecting customary law and land tenure and is authorized to request changes if it feels a bill violates tradition. The *Nitijela* has the legal power to pass any bill it wishes over the council's objections, but it is in fact unlikely to do so when those objections are strong.

3

The Constitution of Palau establishes a Council of Chiefs to advise the elected president of the republic on matters concerning traditional laws and customs. Its power is advisory only, but no president is likely to ignore any strong recommendations the council makes on matters of its special concern.

Article 5 of the Constitution of the Federated States of Micronesia provides that nothing in it "takes away a role or function of a traditional leader as recognized by custom and tradition, or prevents a traditional leader from being recognized, honored, and given formal or functional roles at any level of government." It also authorizes the Congress to establish a chamber of chiefs "when needed." The Congress has not yet done so, but the chiefs continue to play an important role in making political decisions, including the decision on the Compact of Free Association.

Some of the traditional leaders have chosen to participate in the new Western-style governments by running for office or holding appointive positions. For example, Amata Kabua, an *iroij*, has been elected president of the Republic of the Marshall Islands; and the *Ibedul* (paramount chief) Yutaka Gibbons, who was one of the leaders of the organized opposition to the compact in Palau, has been elected governor of the state of Koror. Most traditional leaders, however, have been content to stay out of the new Western-style public politics and to continue their traditional roles. Their leadership had a major impact on the voting in all three 1983 plebiscites. AEI's scholars concluded that one of the most striking characteristics of the plebiscites was the complicated interweaving of Western-style campaigns and elections with the quiet but powerful influence of the traditional leaders.

The Oral Tradition. A third characteristic the Micronesian polities have in common is their traditional reliance on oral rather than on written communications. Illiteracy has been largely eradicated, especially among young people, in recent decades. Even so, most Micronesians of all ages continue to rely more on personal conversations among family members and friends and between traditional chiefs and followers than on newspapers, magazines, letters, or other forms of written communication—including printed translations of the long and legalistic Compact of Free Association.

The Importance of Land Rights. Given that Micronesians live on small dots of land scattered across vast expanses of ocean, it is not surprising that the right to live on, cultivate, and otherwise use a

4

particular piece of land is their prime material value and their first political consideration. As A. John Armstrong states:

> Land in Micronesia is . . . so intimately linked to local politics, economic development and societal ties that the former cannot be separated from the latter. Micronesians identify with their land in a way not known in most Western societies, and Micronesian concepts of land ownership bear scant relationship to those of the United States. For example, a Yapese takes his name, his standing in society and his political power from a tract of land entrusted to him at birth.[3]

As future chapters make clear, issues of the ownership and control of land played major roles in all three 1983 plebiscites. A great concern of most Micronesians is what will happen to the U.S. power of eminent domain. Under the trusteeship system the United States, as the administering authority, exercises a power of eminent domain similar to the power it holds in its own territories: the power to take private land for public use, such as military bases and schools, restricted only by the obligation to pay the owner fair compensation. To many Micronesians this power, which strikes at the very core of their social structure, is the worst part of the trusteeship relation with the United States, and they want to be sure that it will not continue when the trusteeship is terminated.

There have been other special problems. For example, the United States rents land on Kwajalein atoll for the operation of its missile-testing range, and the Micronesian owners of land rights for the sites want to be paid high rents and to be guaranteed that the leases will be renegotiated frequently (see chapter 4). Also, a number of Palauans have been concerned about the possibility that the United States might use Palauan land to construct military facilities, store and transship nuclear materials, and build a super-harbor for oil supertankers. For the Micronesians these issues have been more than merely economic; they touch the very heart of what Micronesians believe are their most basic rights, and it is not surprising that they have aroused more controversy than any other issues.

A Common History of Foreign Rule. Finally, the Micronesians have had a common history of unbroken rule by foreigners since the sixteenth century. Spanish and Portugese explorers first entered the area in that century, and until the late nineteenth century Spain claimed sovereignty over most of the lands and peoples. In 1898 the United States acquired Guam as a result of the Spanish-American war, and in 1899 Spain sold its remaining Micronesian territories to imperial Germany. Early in World War I Japan captured the German-held islands, and in 1920 the League of Nations gave Japan a mandate to administer the Caroline, Marshall, and Northern Mariana islands. From then until the early 1940s the Japanese sent a number of settlers to the islands, developed some economic enterprises, and made a considerable effort to introduce modern methods. Also, they secretly, in violation of their League mandate, fortified several of the islands in preparation for their drive to establish the "greater East Asia co-prosperity sphere." In a series of bloody battles in World War II the armed forces of the United States captured most of the islands and atolls from Japan. In 1947 the United Nations proclaimed most of Micronesia "a strategic trust territory" under the aegis of the Trusteeship Council. The United Nations officially named the area the Trust Territory of the Pacific Islands and designated the United States as the administering authority.

Accordingly, an important question in the 1983 plebiscites was whether accepting the Compact of Free Association with the United States would truly end the centuries of foreign rule of Micronesia and bring its peoples full nationhood or something closely approaching it.

The Micronesian Polities in 1983

While they have many important characteristics in common, Micronesians are also very diverse. For example, at least nine distinct languages are spoken in the area, most with several dialects. Koror in the west is separated from Majuro in the east by 3,940 kilometers of ocean. What is more, the rents received by the Kwajalein landowners are of little concern to the inhabitants of Koror, the question of whether or not a base for nuclear submarines should be built in Palau is of little concern to the residents of Majuro, and the question of whether or not the Faichuks should be independent of Truk stirs little discussion in Jaluit. Most important, the events of the 1970s and 1980s made it clear that there is little, if any, area-wide sense of cultural or political identity that can be described as "Micronesian nationalism" and little political activity that can be called "Micronesian solidarity." On the contrary, the geographical area called Micronesia has, in accordance with the wishes of its various peoples, become divided into the following four distinct political entities, three of which held plebiscites in 1983.

The Commonwealth of the Northern Mariana Islands. The Commonwealth of the Northern Mariana Islands[4] consists of a group of sixteen islands, the most important of which are Saipan, Tinian, and Rota. The capital is located on Saipan. Together these islands have a total land mass of 479 square kilometers, and the population is estimated to be about 16,800. The official languages are English and Chamorro.

In the early 1970s several political leaders in the Northern Marianas decided that they wanted closer post-trusteeship relations with the United States than the Trust Territory's other jurisdictions appeared to want, so they asked that their future status be negotiated separately from the others. The United States granted their request. In a 1975 plebiscite the people of the Northern Marianas voted, by a majority of 78.5 percent, to become a U.S. "commonwealth"—a status similar, but not identical, to that of Puerto Rico. The new status was approved by the U.S. Congress and went into effect in 1976. Strictly speaking, the Northern Marianas are still part of the Trust Territory and will remain so until the trusteeship is terminated for the entire territory. Since 1976, however, they have had a larger degree of self-government than the other jurisdictions.

The Northern Marianas have a "presidential" form of democracy based upon separation of powers and modeled on the government of the United States. The legislative power is vested in the bicameral Northern Marianas Commonwealth Legislature: the Senate has nine members elected at large from the three senatorial districts for four-year terms, and the House of Representatives has fourteen members elected for two-year terms. The executive power is located in the governor, who is directly elected for a four-year term and who serves as chief executive. The judicial authority rests in the Commonwealth Trial Court, which has original jurisdiction over land disputes and other civil questions. Criminal matters are adjudicated by the U.S. courts.

The Republic of Palau. Westernmost of the Micronesian jurisdictions, the Republic of Palau consists of more than two hundred islands, only eight of which are inhabited. The total land mass is 492 square kilometers, only slightly larger than that of the Northern Marianas. Palau is divided into sixteen localities which formerly had the status of municipalities but which became states under the 1980 constitution. Ten are located on the main island of Babelthuap (which has the largest land area), and the most distant are Tobi (560 kilometers from Koror) and Sonsorol (320 kilometers). The national capital is located on the island of Koror. The total population is estimated to be 12,100 and the four official languages are English, Palauan, Tobian, and Sonsorolese. In the 1978 referendum on the proposed constitution to unite all the Micronesian territories except the Northern

7

Marianas under one federation, the people of Palau voted to reject federation and form their own polity. They approved a new constitution for themselves in a 1979 referendum, and in 1981 the newly elected government took office. This government conducted the 1983 plebiscite on the Compact of Free Association.

The 1980 Palau constitution places the legislative power in the *Olbiil Era Kelulau* (OEK), a bicameral legislature. The House of Delegates is composed of one delegate elected from each state, and the Senate is composed of senators elected from districts apportioned, from time to time, by a reapportionment commission. The executive authority is vested in a president, who is directly elected for a four-year term. The president of Palau, like the president of the United States, is authorized to veto bills passed by the legislature, but, as in the United States, his veto may be overridden by a two-thirds vote in each of the legislature's two chambers. The judicial power is vested in a unified national judiciary consisting of a Supreme Court, a National Court, and some inferior courts of limited jurisdiction established by the OEK. Thus Palau, like the Northern Marianas, has a presidential form of democracy based upon separation of powers.

The Federated States of Micronesia. In both land area and population the Federated States of Micronesia (FSM) is the largest of the four Trust Territory jurisdictions. It consists of the four districts of the Trust Territory—Kosrae, Ponape, Truk, and Yap—whose voters in the 1978 referendum approved the proposed constitution for the Micronesia-wide federation. Currently each of the four states has its own constitution and elected legislature and governor. Each state also sends elected representatives to the one-house federal Congress, which sits in the national capital located in the town of Kolonia on the island of Ponape. Each state is entitled to one member elected for a four-year term and to four additional members, each elected for a two-year term, apportioned according to population. The executive power is vested in the president of the federation, who is chosen by the Congress from among its four-year members. The president serves a four-year term and may serve no more than two consecutive terms. The vice-president, although elected in the same manner as the president, may not be a citizen of the same state as the president. The FSM's judicial power is vested in a Supreme Court and in inferior courts as established by the Congress. Thus the FSM's constitutional system is something of a hybrid: the chief executive is selected by the legislature from among its own members, but once he becomes president he is no longer a member of the Congress and operates as an independent executive. Perhaps "quasi-presidential" is the best label for the FSM's system.

The total population of the FSM is about 73,200. Truk, with 37,500, is the most populous of its states, followed by Ponape with 22,100, Yap with 8,100, and Kosrae with 5,500. Linguistically it is by far the most diverse of all the Micronesian polities. The federation has nine official languages: English, Ponapean, Trukese, Kosraean, Yapese, Nukuoran, Kapingi, Ulithian, and Wolian. Some of its constituent parts, notably Ponape and the Faichuk Islands in Truk state, harbor strong separatist sentiments, which played prominent roles in the 1983 plebiscites and pose problems for the federation's future. There are territorial antagonisms within all of the Micronesian polities, but they are strongest in the FSM.

The Republic of the Marshall Islands. The Republic of the Marshall Islands is the easternmost of the Micronesian jurisdictions. It consists of twenty-nine coral atolls and five coral islands dispersed over 970,000 square kilometers of ocean. The total land mass, however, is only 180 square kilometers, the smallest of any of the four polities. The islands form two chains: the Ratak (sunrise) chain to the east and the Ralik (sunset) chain to the west. The total population is estimated to be 31,000, and the two main population centers are the atolls of Majuro (10,000), in which the capital is located, and Kwajalein, in which the most populous island is Ebeye (8,500). The official languages are English and Marshallese. On several islands in Kwajalein atoll, mainly Kwajalein, Roi-Namur, and Carlos, the United States operates the Kwajalein Missile Range (KMR) for testing intercontinental ballistic missiles launched from Vandenberg Air Force Base in California. The land is rented from Micronesians who have land rights in the atoll but for the most part are residents of Ebeye. In the 1978 referendum the people of the Marshall Islands joined the people of Palau in rejecting inclusion in a Micronesia-wide political entity. In a 1979 referendum they approved a new constitution for their own area, and the newly elected government for the Republic of the Marshall Islands took office on May 1, 1979.

The 1979 Marshallese constitution vests legislative power in the *Nitijela* (parliament), which is composed of thirty-three members elected for four-year terms from single-member districts throughout the islands. As in the FSM, the *Nitijela* chooses one of its own members as president, and he serves as chief executive and head of state. Unlike the presidents of Palau or the FSM, however, the president of the Marshall Islands is required to resign when a majority of the

Nitijela votes no confidence in him. The president also has the power under certain conditions to dissolve the *Nitijela* and call new elections. Thus the Marshall Islands has essentially a parliamentary form of democracy influenced more by the Westminster model than by the Washington model.

These, then, are the four Micronesian polities that existed in 1983. Their emergence from the original Trust Territory districts and the political evolution leading to the 1983 plebiscites are best understood in the light of the following brief summary of developments after the end of World War II.

A Brief History of the Trust Territory of the Pacific Islands

Establishment and Terms. As we noted earlier, most of the islands, atolls, and peoples of Micronesia were under Japanese rule from 1914 until World War II, when they were captured, at great cost in lives and treasure, by the armed forces of the United States. In 1946 the United States agreed to place the captured Micronesian territories under the International Trusteeship System of the United Nations. In 1947 the United Nations Security Council and the United States Congress approved the Trusteeship Agreement for the Trust Territory of the Pacific Islands, which, under Article 76 of the United Nations Charter, declared the area to be a "strategic trust" with the United States as the administering authority. This particular form of trusteeship, the only one established by the United Nations, was created to accommodate the position of the United States that Micronesia's strategic location makes it of special importance for the maintenance of international peace and security. Thus Micronesia was to be treated differently from the ten other territories that were placed under the trusteeship of various UN members during the same period.

Under the 1947 Trusteeship Agreement, the United States assumed certain rights and obligations, of which the most significant were the following:[5]

- to "foster the development of such political institutions as are suited to the trust territory and [to] promote the development of the inhabitants of the trust territory toward self-government or independence as may be appropriate to the particular circumstances of the trust territory and its peoples and the freely expressed wishes of the peoples concerned"
- to "promote the economic advancement and self-sufficiency of the inhabitants"

10

- to "promote the social advancement of the inhabitants [and] protect the rights and fundamental freedoms of all elements of the populations without discrimination"
- to "promote the educational advancement of the inhabitants"
- to "establish naval, military and air bases . . . , to station and employ armed forces in the territory . . . , [and] to make use of volunteer forces, facilities and assistance from the trust territory in carrying out the obligations undertaken . . . by the administering authority, as well as for the local defense and maintenance of law and order within the trust territory"

Evolution of the Districts. From its establishment in 1947 until the mid-1970s, the Trust Territory was divided into six districts. The original districts were the Northern Marianas, the Marshall Islands, Palau, Ponape, Truk, and Yap. During most of this period the United States tried to encourage the districts to unite in one Micronesia-wide federation with which negotiations for the area's post-trusteeship status could be conducted. That policy, however, failed under the pressures of the territory's various separationist movements.

The first crack in Micronesian unity appeared in the early 1970s when, as noted earlier, the Northern Marianas insisted that they wanted closer relations with the United States than the other districts wanted and asked not to be included in any Micronesia-wide political entity. Shortly after the Northern Marianas were given de facto commonwealth status in 1976, the island of Kosrae asked for and was given full district status, and joined Palau, the Marshalls, Ponape, Truk, and Yap as the districts whose future status was yet to be determined.

On several occasions in the 1970s the Marshallese *Nitijela* adopted resolutions informing the United States and the United Nations that they, too, wanted a status separate from that of the other districts. In 1977 the Marshalls held a plebiscite asking their people whether they approved of the movement to seek separate status, and 82 percent voted their approval.

The district of Palau also sought separation from the other districts. In 1977 the United States finally yielded to the Marshallese and Palauan separationist sentiments by agreeing to conduct "two-tiered" negotiations on the future status of the Trust Territory districts. One tier was to be multilateral negotiatins with the six districts on the matters that were common to all—for example, defense, foreign relations, and the concept of "free association." The other tier was to be bilateral negotiations between the United States and Palau, the

11

United States and the Marshall Islands, and the United States and the Ponape-Truk-Yap-Kosrae group.

A constitutional convention composed of delegates from each of the six districts prepared a constitution for a "federated states of Micronesia," and a referendum was held in each of the six districts on July 12, 1978, under the inspection of a team of observers sent by the United Nations Trusteeship Council. The results of the referendum are shown in table 1–1:

TABLE 1–1

RESULTS OF THE 1978 REFERENDUM ON THE
PROPOSED ALL-MICRONESIA FEDERATION CONSTITUTION

| District | Registered Voters | Votes Cast | % Turnout | % Voting | |
				Yes	No
Marshall Islands	12,996	10,105	77.8	38.5	61.5
Palau	6,500	6,059	93.2	44.9	55.1
Ponape	11,177	7,990	71.5	74.7	25.3
Truk	17,736	14,001	78.9	69.7	30.3
Yap	4,650	3,545	76.2	94.8	5.2
Kosrae	2,182	1,822	83.5	61.4	38.6
Total	55,241	43,522	78.8	61.6	38.4

SOURCE: *Report of the United Nations Visiting Mission to Observe the Referendum in the Trust Territory of the Pacific Islands, 1978* (UN Document T/1795, 1979), p. 57

The enabling legislation for the 1978 referendum stipulated that at least four of the six districts had to approve the constitution for it to go into effect. The legislation also guaranteed that no district would be included in the federation if its people did not approve the proposed constitution. As table 1–1 shows, the constitution was approved by the voters of Ponape, Truk, Yap, and Kosrae but disapproved by the voters of Palau and the Marshall Islands. Accordingly, the first four districts became the four states of the Federated States of Micronesia, and the FSM's newly elected officers took office in 1979.

As noted earlier, in 1979 the Marshall Islands adopted its own constitution and installed its own government. In 1981 Palau followed suit. In this manner the original six districts of the Trust Territory and the added district of Kosrae were, by 1981, sorted out into the four political entities described above, three of which in 1983 held plebiscites on the proposed Compact of Free Association with the United States.

U.S. Administration of the Trust Territory. From 1947 to 1951 the U.S. government assigned responsibility for administering the affairs of the Trust Territory to the Department of the Navy. In 1951 the main administrative responsibility was transferred to the Department of the Interior, and by 1982–1983 the principal agency supervising the territory was the Office of the Assistant Secretary of the Interior for Territorial and International Affairs. At the time of the plebiscites the assistant secretary in charge was Pedro A. Sanjuan. The chief administrative officer, with offices located in Saipan, was High Commissioner Janet McCoy, who was appointed by the president and confirmed by the Senate.

Under the trusteeship agreement the United States has the full power of administration, legislation, and adjudication over all territories and peoples in the Trust Territory. Since the mid-1970s, however, the area's four jurisdictions have acquired considerable degrees of self-government. Although the ultimate legal powers will remain with the United States until the trusteeship is terminated by the United Nations, most of the functions previously performed by the office of the high commissioner have devolved upon the new constitutional governments of the four polities. The high commissioner retains the power to suspend, in whole or in part, laws adopted by any of the four governments that conflict with the administering authority's responsibilities under the trusteeship agreement, but this power is seldom used. Accordingly, each of the three plebiscites described in this report was conducted according to the laws and administrative procedures adopted and administered, not by the United States, but by the government of the Micronesian polity concerned—a point worth remembering when, in subsequent chapters, we review the conduct of the plebiscites.

Development of Self-Government, 1947–1983.

District Legislatures. As we noted earlier, one obligation assumed by the United States under the trusteeship agreement has been to foster the development of political institutions in the territory leading to self-government. The United States has undertaken several efforts to that end. One of the earliest efforts was encouraging the districts to establish their own elected legislatures to exercise the powers devolved to the districts by the United States—notably, the power to make laws governing the districts' internal affairs.

Palau established the first district legislature in 1947, and similar legislatures were established in the Marshall Islands (1950), in Truk (1957), in Ponape (1958), in Yap (1959), and in the Northern Marianas (1963). The legislatures of Palau, the Marshall Islands, Ponape, and Truk all appointed commissions to conduct negotiations with the United States about their post-territory status. All the district legislatures exerted considerable power over their own internal affairs, and they also served as training grounds for many of Micronesia's future political leaders.

The Congress of Micronesia, 1965–1978. The most important agency of area-wide self-government before the political fragmentation of the mid-1970s was the Congress of Micronesia (COM). It played a major role in the early negotiations over the future status of the Trust Territory, and most of its leading members became leaders of the four emerging polities.

The Charter for the Congress of Micronesia was drawn up from 1962 to 1965 in discussions among representatives from the Trust Territory districts and from the Office of Territories in the U.S. Department of the Interior. An order by the secretary of the interior in 1965 established the Congress as a bicameral body, consisting of a Senate and a House of Representatives. The Senate had twelve members, with two elected at large from each of the six districts. The House of Representatives had twenty-one members elected for two-year terms from single-member constituencies apportioned among the districts as follows:

Truk	5
Marshall Islands	4
Ponape	4
Northern Marianas	3
Palau	3
Yap	2

The first congressional election was the first election held in the whole Trust Territory. It began on December 28, 1964, and ended on January 27, 1965. The fact that it took a month to cast, collect, and count all the ballots dramatically signaled the difficulties of holding an election among so few voters scattered over such vast distances. The turnout figures summarized in table 1–2 provide a benchmark against which to compare turnouts in the subsequent elections in the area, including the 1983 plebiscites. Those figures represent an impressive performance by the Micronesian people in their first full-scale democratic election ever. Micronesians' participation in subsequent elections, including the 1983 plebiscites, has also been high and is especially remarkable in view of the great logistical difficulties.

TABLE 1–2

TRUST TERRITORY TURNOUT IN THE 1965 ELECTIONS FOR THE CONGRESS OF MICRONESIA

District	Estimated Persons Eligible to Vote	Persons Voting	% Turnout
Truk	12,255	5,373	43.8
Ponape	9,200	5,637	61.3
Marshall Islands	8,000	4,218	52.7
Palau	4,654	3,711	79.7
Northern Marianas	4,104	3,356	81.8
Yap	3,290	2,767	84.1
Total	41,503	25,062	60.4

SOURCE: Norman Meller, *The Congress of Micronesia* (Honolulu: University of Hawaii Press, 1969), p. 271.

More than three-quarters of the members of the Congress of Micronesia elected in 1965 and in subsequent elections (a total of seven were held in even-numbered years from 1966 to 1978) had served as members of the district legislatures, and several became prominent figures in the post-1978 constitutional governments. For example, one of Micronesia's leading statesmen, Tosiwo Nakayama of Truk, was elected president of the COM Senate and later became president of the Federated States of Micronesia. Amata Kabua of the Marshall Islands became chairman of the COM House of Representative's Committee on Ways and Means and later became president of the Republic of the Marshall Islands. Bethwel Henry of Ponape became secretary of the COM House of Representatives and later the speaker of the FSM Congress.

The Charter of the Congress gave the COM full authority over "all rightful subjects of legislation, except that no such legislation may be inconsistent with (a) treaties or international agreements of the United States, (b) laws of the United States applicable to the Trust Territory, or (c) sections 1 through 12 of the Code of the Trust Territory." The high commissioner retained the power to veto any act of Congress deemed to transgress these limits, but the power was rarely used.

The Congress of Micronesia first convened on July 12, 1965, and for the next decade it was the main agency of local self-government for the Trust Territory as a whole. Moreover, one of its committees took a major part in the long series of negotiations leading to the Compact of Free Association with the United States.

By order of the secretary of the interior on October 2, 1978, the Congress of Micronesia was dissolved and its powers were assumed by the legislatures of Palau, the FSM, and the Marshall Islands.

Evolution of the Compact of Free Association, 1969–1983. On August 8, 1967, the Congress of Micronesia established a Joint Committee on Future Political Status, with one representative from each Trust Territory district, and with Lazarus Salii, a member of the COM House of Representatives from Palau, as chairman. The commission's final report, issued in July 1969, became the first major event in the evolution of the Compact of Free Association. The report recommended that the future status of the Trust Territory should be governed by four precepts: 1. sovereignty in Micronesia should rest in the Micronesian people and their duly constituted government or governments; 2. the people of Micronesia by right have the power of self-determination and may, therefore, choose independence or self-government in free association with any nation or organization of nations; 3. the people of Micronesia have the right to adopt their own constitution and amend, change, or revoke any constitution at any time; and 4. free association should take the form of a revocable compact that can be terminated unilaterally by either party.

The commission's report launched serious negotiations between the Micronesian leaders and representatives of the United States. These negotiations began in 1969 and ended in 1982, when the United States and the Marshall Islands (May 30), the United States and Palau (August 26), and the United States and the Federated States of Micronesia (October 1) signed the Compact of Free Association and various related agreements. Each of the Micronesian polities agreed to hold plebiscites in 1983 seeking popular approval of the terms negotiated by the government. In December 1982 the Trusteeship Council of the United Nations agreed to send visiting missions to observe each of the three plebiscites.

The story of the thirteen years of negotiations leading to the events of 1982–1983 is far too complex to be told in detail here, but a few of the highlights should be noted.

16

During the beginning stages in 1969–1970 the United States offered the districts the post-trusteeship status of being U.S. territories, but the Micronesians rejected the offer. Their principal objection was that such status would continue the United States' power of eminent domain over Micronesian land. Securing Micronesian control of Micronesian land was, and remains, a prime value for the Micronesians.

The United States then offered commonwealth status along the general lines established for Puerto Rico. This offer was welcomed by the Northern Marianas but rejected by the other districts. In 1971 the U.S. and Micronesian negotiators agreed upon the principle of "free association," which in general entailed the Micronesians' having full authority over their own internal affairs, including the control of land rights, and the United States government's retaining authority over defense and foreign affairs and continuing economic support of Micronesia.

In 1975 the district of the Northern Marianas voted to separate itself from the other Trust Territory districts and to enter into a Covenant to Establish a Commonwealth of the Northern Mariana Islands in Political Union with the United States of America. The covenant was approved by the Northern Marianas voters in a plebiscite observed and approved by representatives of the United Nations Trusteeship Council. It was enacted into law by the U.S. Congress in 1976 and went into force on January 9, 1978.

The negotiations between the United States and the remaining Trust Territory districts (which became six again in 1977 when Kosrae was given district status) followed a tortuous path during much of the 1970s. One breakthrough occurred in 1973 when the United States agreed that all Micronesian public lands would be transferred to local control and that the U.S. power of eminent domain would end when the trusteeship was terminated. Disagreements continued regarding the level of funding that the United States would guarantee to the districts after the end of the trusteeship. There were also disagreements about such matters as U.S. liability for injuries to individuals resulting from their relocation and from fallout generated by the test explosions of nuclear weapons in parts of the Marshall Islands in 1951.

After 1977 the United States reluctantly accepted the political fragmentation of Micronesia into four separate jurisdictions and agreed to conduct "two-tiered" negotiations. Perhaps the most important breakthrough was achieved during meetings in Hilo, Hawaii, in 1978. Micronesian and American negotiators agreed on eight basic principles that would shape the eventual compacts of free association. For present purposes the most important of the principles were the following:

 • The peoples of Micronesia will enjoy full internal self-government.
 • The United States will have full authority and responsibility for security and defense matters in or relating to Micronesia, including the establishment of necessary military facilities and the exercise of appropriate operating rights. The peoples of Micronesia will refrain from actions which the United States determines, after appropriate consultations, to be incompatible with its authority and responsibility for security and defense matters in or relating to Micronesia. This authority and responsibility will be assured for fifteen years, and thereafter as mutually agreed. Specific land arrangements will remain in effect according to terms which will be negotiated prior to the end of the Trusteeship Agreement.
 • The peoples of Micronesia will have authority and responsibility for their foreign affairs, including marine resources. They will consult with the United States in the exercise of this authority and will refrain from actions which the United States determines to be incompatible with its authority and responsibility for security and defense matters in or relating to Micronesia. The United States may act on behalf of the peoples of Micronesia in the area of foreign affairs as mutually agreed from time to time.
 • The agreement will permit unilateral termination of the free association political status by the same processes through which it was entered and set forth in the agreement, and subject to the continuation of United States defense authority and responsibility; but any plebiscite terminating the free association status will not require observation by the United Nations.
 • Should the free association status be mutually terminated, the United States economic assistance shall continue as mutually agreed. Should the United States terminate the free association relationship, its economic assistance to Micronesia shall continue at the levels and for the term initially agreed. If the agreement is otherwise terminated, the United States shall no longer be obligated to provide the same amounts of economic assistance for the remainder of the term initially agreed.[6]

On the basis of the Hilo principles, a compact of free association and a set of related agreements were worked out for each of the three jurisdictions. Approval of those compacts and related agreements constituted the questions voted on in the 1983 plebiscites.

An Outline of the Compact of Free Association. Before considering the Compact of Free Association in some detail, it may be useful to note A. John Armstrong's succinct statement of its essential principles:

> Free association differs from independence in that one of the parties to the bilateral agreement willingly binds itself, by its own constitutional processes . . . to cede to the other a fundamental sovereign authority and responsibility for the conduct of its own affairs. Specifically, this distinction is exemplified by the reservation to the United States of plenary defense authority (as contrasted with treaty rights to exercise certain defense functions), and the ensuing limitation on Micronesian freedom of action. Free association is distinguished from integration into a metropolitan power by the retention by the freely associated government of the power to assert itself domestically and internationally without reference to the legal authority of another state.[7]

To set forth the main provisions of the compact, we shall use the one signed by the United States and the Federated States of Micronesia and approved by the people of the FSM in the plebiscite of June 21, 1983. That compact is a long and complex document. It contains a total of four titles and twenty-four articles. The English language version occupies 243 single-spaced pages. Accordingly, we shall present only an outline of its main provisions.

Title One: Governmental Relations. The people of the Federated States of Micronesia, acting through the government established by their constitution, are self-governing. The FSM retains full authority over its internal affairs. The government of the FSM has the capacity to conduct foreign affairs and shall do so in its own name and right, including entering into treaties and other international agreements with governments and regional and international organizations. In recognition of the authority and responsibility of the United States under Title Three, the government of the FSM shall consult, in the conduct of the FSM's foreign affairs, with the government of the United States (but only on defense and security matters does the United States retain the power to veto proposed actions by the FSM). Any citizen of the FSM can enter the United States and reside and work there as a nonimmigrant for an indefinite period. Citizens of the

FSM are not citizens of the United States. Citizens or nationals of the United States may reside and work in the FSM subject to the right of the FSM government to deny entry to or deport any such persons as undesirable aliens. U.S. laws cease to have effect in the FSM when the compact goes into effect.

Title Two: Economic Relations. The United States government agrees to pay to the government of the FSM $60 million annually for five years commencing on the effective date of the compact, $51 million annually for the succeeding five years, and $40 million annually for the five years after that—for a total of $755 million over fifteen years. The FSM agrees to spend not less than 40 percent of this money on economic development. The FSM national government will divide funds among the four states of the FSM. The FSM will report to the president and the Congress of the United States annually on how the FSM's development plan is being implemented and on how the development funds are being spent. The United States will provide additional annual contributions for such purposes as the development of communications, scholarships, and operation of U.S. military and meteorological stations. The FSM government may tax any U.S. citizen for income derived within the FSM. The U.S. government may not tax FSM citizens for income derived in either the FSM or the United States.

Title Three: Security and Defense Relations. The United States has full authority and responsibility for security and defense matters in or relating to the FSM. This responsibility includes an obligation to defend the FSM, an option to foreclose access to the FSM for military forces of a third country, and an option to establish or use military facilities and conduct military operations in the FSM, subject to certain agreed limitations. The FSM agrees to refrain from activities that the United States, after consultation with the FSM, determines to be incompatible with defense. Testing of nuclear weapons, dumping of nuclear or radioactive wastes, and storage of nuclear weapons or other nuclear materials are prohibited except in emergencies and by mutual agreement between the United States and the FSM. The United States and the FSM will establish a joint committee to consider any disputes arising under this title and subsidiary agreements. Any citizen of the FSM is eligible to serve in the U.S. armed forces but is not subject to any military draft by the United States. The United States cannot include the FSM in any declaration of war without the FSM's consent. The provisions of this title are binding from the effective date of the compact for a period of fifteen years and thereafter as mutually agreed unless terminated or amended earlier by mutual agreement.

Title Four: General Provisions. The compact will take effect on a date agreed upon by the United States and the FSM after the completion of three steps: 1. approval by a majority of the people of the FSM voting in a plebiscite; 2. approval by the constitutional processes of the FSM, including approval by the legislatures of at least three of the four states and approval by a two-thirds vote of the FSM Congress; and 3. approval by the United States through its constitutional processes, including Congress's adoption of appropriate laws that are then signed by the president. An arbitration board will be established to deal with disputes arising under titles 1, 2, and 4. The United States can terminate the compact by an act of Congress signed by the president. The FSM Congress can terminate the compact after a plebiscite approving termination.

The Related Agreements. The people of the FSM voted to approve or disapprove the Compact of Free Association "and its related agreements." The contents of those agreements are indicated by their titles: 1 and 2. Telecommunications; 3. Marine Sovereignty; 4. Law Enforcement and Extradition; 5. Federal Programs and Services; 6. Property Transfer; 7. Military Use and Operating Rights; 8. Status of Forces; and 9. Friendship, Cooperation and Mutual Security.

The last of these agreements contained the principle of "long-term denial" of access to the FSM's territory and waters by the armed forces of any third country, which most negotiators for both the United States and FSM regarded as the core of the proposed new relationship. According to article IV of the agreement:

> 2. If the Government of the United States determines that any third country seeks access to or use of the Federated States of Micronesia by military personnel or for military puposes, the Government of the United States has the authority and responsibility to foreclose such access or use, except in instances where the two Governments otherwise agree.

The Importance of the Plebiscites. One final point should be noted about the Compact of Free Association and the processes by which it was negotiated. The one matter of universal agreement was that any post-trusteeship status negotiated for any of the Trust Territory's districts must accord with *the freely-expressed wishes of the people concerned*—a phrase that occurs again and again in the position papers and other documents of the negotiations. That principle, it was further agreed, would be implemented in two ways. First, the negotiations for each Micronesian polity would be conducted by persons chosen by and answerable to the freely elected government of that polity. Second, whatever status was negotiated and approved by the government of each polity required the approval of a majority of the polity's voters in a free and democratic plebiscite. Thus the United Nations Trusteeship Council sent teams of observers to every major plebiscite, beginning with the one on the establishment of commonwealth status for the Northern Marianas in 1975 to the three plebiscites on the Compact of Free Association and related agreements in 1983.

We turn now to descriptions and analyses of the laws, administrative rules, politics, outcomes, and consequences of the plebiscites conducted in February, June, and September of 1983.

NOTES

1. *The Times* (London), September 14, 1983.
2. For details, see the annual reports of the Trust Territory of the Pacific Islands to the United States secretary of the interior.
3. Arthur John Armstrong, "The Emergence of the Micronesians into the International Community: A Study of the Creation of a New International Entity," *Brooklyn Journal of International Law*, vol. 5 (1979), pp. 218–19.
4. Useful brief descriptions of the constitutional systems of the Micronesian polities are given in *Outline of Conditions in the Trust Territory of the Pacific Islands* (UN document T/L. 1235, 1983), pp. 8–16.
5. The text is printed in *1983: Trust Territory of the Pacific Islands* (Washington, D.C.: Thirty-sixth Annual Report by the United States to the United Nations on the Administration of the Trust Territory of the Pacific Islands, 1983), pp. 215–28.
6. The Hilo principles are printed in Armstrong, "The Emergence of the Micronesians," pp. 260–61.
7. Arthur John Armstrong, "Strategic Underpinnings of the Legal Regime of Free Association: The Negotiations for the Future Political Status of Micronesia," *Brooklyn Journal of International Law*, vol. 7 (1981), p. 182.

The Republic of Palau

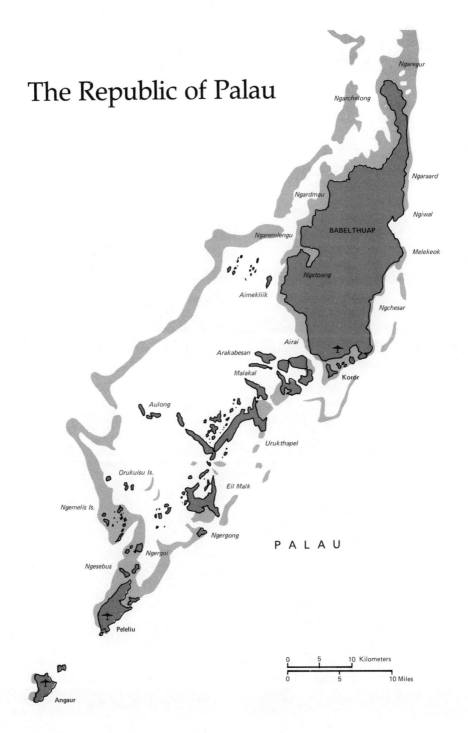

Ngaregur

Ngarchelong

Ngaraard

Ngardmau

Ngiwal

Ngaremlengu

BABELTHUAP

Melekeok

Ngatpang

Ngchesar

Aimekliik

Airai

Arakabesan

Malakal

Korór

Aulong

Urukthapel

Orukuisu Is.

Eil Malk

Ngemelis Is.

Ngergong

PALAU

Ngergoi

Ngesebus

Peleliu

| 0 | 5 | 10 Kilometers |
| 0 | 5 | 10 Miles |

Angaur

2

The Republic of Palau

The plebiscite in the Republic of Palau received special attention in late 1982 and early 1983 for several reasons. First, it was the earliest held, and officials in New York and Washington as well as in Ponape and Majuro hoped Palau's experience would alert them to problems and possibilities of holding the future plebiscites in the FSM and the Marshall Islands. Second, some partisans hoped that a vote in favor of the compact in Palau would, by some kind of transoceanic bandwagon effect, boost the chances for passage in the FSM and the Marshalls; and other partisans hoped that defeating the compact in Palau would make it easier to defeat elsewhere. Third, since the late 1960s one of the most prominent Micronesian spokesmen in the negotiations with the United States about the compact's terms had been the Palauan senator Lazarus H. Salii; holding the first plebiscite in his home territory seemed not only appropriate but perhaps also indicative of how the political trade wind was blowing.

In the event, Palau's plebiscite was indeed noteworthy, but for somewhat differerent reasons. At almost every stage of the process there was strong and often acrimonious controversy. Many non-Palauan organizations and individuals, including some from the United States, were active in funding and organizing campaigns. The outcome was an unusual and, to many, vexing mixture of a reasonably strong majority for most of the compact and a narrow—and constitutionally insufficient—majority for the section regarding storage and transshipment of nuclear weapons. An interpretation of the results by Palau's Supreme Court made Palau the only jurisdiction not to ratify the compact. The story is absorbing, and we shall tell it in some detail.

AEI's team of scholars for the plebiscite in the Republic of Palau consisted of Alan Cairns, Howard Penniman, and Richard Smolka.

Penniman and Smolka went to Palau on October 1–8, 1982, and again on November 18–27, 1982. All three went to Palau on February 3–16, 1983.

During the first two visits the scholars engaged in discussions with the Palauan officials in charge of conducting the political education program and the plebiscite. These officials included Daiziro Nakamura, director of the Bureau of Domestic Affairs, who served as the chief administrator for the plebiscite; Bonifacio Basilius, chief of the Division of Public Affairs, who was especially concerned with the political education program; and Mamoru Nakamura, the chief justice, who made some important rulings about the wording of the ballot.

A second set of discussions was held with leaders of the government who had negotiated the compact and supported it. These included President Haruo Remeliik and Vice-President Alfonso Oiterong, Ambassador Lazarus H. Salii, Acting Chief Reklai Termeteet, and Carlos H. Salii, the speaker of the lower house of the *Olbiil Era Kelulau* (OEK—the Palauan Congress).

A third set of discussions was held with the leaders of the opposition to the compact, mainly Senators Moses Uludong, Johnson Toribiong, and Joshua Koshiba, and the Ibedul, Yutaka Gibbons, the governor of the state of Koror.

The AEI scholars also met with the chiefs and other officials of six villages on the east side of the main island of Babelthuap, traveling from point to point by boat because ground transportation was too difficult. They attended several meetings in which representatives of the political education program discussed with the villagers the provisions, merits, and demerits of the compact. Perhaps the most interesting of these meetings was conducted in Koror by the Ibedul, Yutaka Gibbons, who is not only the governor of the state of Koror but also the paramount chief in the traditional social structure. All the lesser chiefs in the Ibedul's clan attended. The Ibedul made clear his strong opposition to the compact, and the other chiefs all publicly supported his position. The AEI scholars' guide, a young man who had studied at the University of Arkansas, was the son of one of the lesser chiefs. His father was a strong supporter of the compact, but at the meeting he publicly supported the Ibedul's position. He later explained that when one is a guest of the high chief one must not insult him by publicly taking an opposing position. This incident was one of many manifesting the importance of the traditional chiefs in the discussions and voting, a pattern that was significant not only in Palau but in the FSM and the Marshall Islands as well.

Posters in Palauan and English were mounted throughout Koror and elsewhere. The procompact posters stressed the necessity of defending Palau against Soviet aggression.

Above left: Anticompact posters emphasized the need to keep nuclear materials out of Palauan territory. Above right: In Palau all polling places were indoors, and voters deposited their marked ballots in double-lidded ballot boxes similar to those used in the FSM and the Marshall Islands and to the one pictured on the cover.

Most of the voter education meetings were held in open-air meeting places with tented roofs. This meeting in Koror was called by the paramount chief, the Ibedul Yutaka Gibbons, and the traditional respect for his position was manifested by the lesser chiefs' reluctance to oppose publicly his stand against the compact.

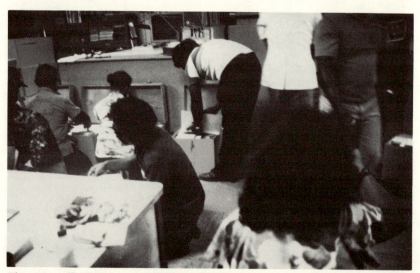

The voting officials were carefully trained in election procedures in sessions conducted by Daiziro Nakamura, chairman of the Plebiscite Commission. When their training was completed they were sent to the villages, where they presided over the casting of the ballots.

Preliminaries to the Plebiscite

Palauan Separatism. Palauan separatism[1] first surfaced in 1973 when the legislature of the Palau district of the Trust Territory adopted several resolutions calling for a status separate from that of other parts of Micronesia. On July 8, 1975, an advisory referendum regarding the post-trusteeship status of Micronesia was held in all parts of the Trust Territory in which the voters were asked to express their preferences for alternatives including independence, commonwealth, statehood, free association, or a continuation of the trusteeship. Palauan voters voted 1,288 for continuing the trusteeship and 1,120 for free association.

Though the vote was extremely close, the Palauan legislature evidently felt that it indicated sufficient sentiment for separate treatment to proceed with a second referendum. The question was whether or not Palau's future status should be determined by negotiations with the United States separate from those being conducted with other parts of Micronesia. The second referendum was held on September 24, 1976, and 88.5 percent of the voters voted in favor of separate negotiations, while only 11.5 percent voted for unified negotiations.

The next vote was a July 12, 1978, referendum on the proposed constitution for a federated government for Palau and the other Trust Territory districts. Palauans voted 2,720 (44.9 percent) for the constitution and 3,339 (55.1 percent) against it. The defeat of the constitution in Palau and in the Marshall Islands, as we have already noted, led the United States to accept the principle of separate, two-tiered negotiations. Since then Palau has been accorded a status separate from that of Micronesia's other jurisdictions.

A Palauan constitutional convention then drafted a proposed constitution for the Republic of Palau, providing for a president directly elected by the people for a four-year term, a separate two-house Congress (the OEK) and an independent, appointed judiciary—in short, a presidential system modeled upon that of the United States rather than a parliamentary system as adopted by the Marshall Islands. In a referendum held on July 9, 1979, Palau's voters voted 4,023 (92.0 percent) in favor of the proposed constitution to 349 (8.0 percent) against. The officials elected and appointed under this new constitution prescribed and administered the rules under which the 1983 plebiscite was conducted.

The Draft Compact and Agreements. The draft Compact of Free Association and related agreements between the Republic of Palau and the United States of America was initialed by representatives of the two parties on November 17, 1980. After President Ronald Reagan took office on January 20, 1981, his administration reviewed the status of the Micronesian negotiations and decided to proceed with plebiscites on the Compact of Free Association in all three Trust Territory jurisdictions as soon as possible. The negotiations were resumed, some revisions were made in both the compact and the related agreements, and the new versions were signed by the Palauan and U.S. negotiators on August 26, 1982.

The compact for Palau was essentially the same as that for each of the other two jurisdictions (its main provisions are outlined in chapter 1). There were also six multilateral related agreements that were the same for all three jurisdictions. In addition, five bilateral related agreements for Palau covered the following matters:

• the management of the funds to be provided for Palau by the United States

• construction projects to be financed by the United States, including a new road for Babelthuap

• in pursuance of sections 321 and 323 of the compact, an agreement by Palau to give the United States the option to use four sites in Palau for construction of defense facilities

• a clarification of the language of section 314 of the compact regarding the status of radioactive, chemical, and biological substances (which became the main issue in the plebiscite campaign)

• a statement guaranteeing Palau's sovereignty over its territory, including its land, internal waters, territorial seas, and superadjacent airspace

The Timing of the Plebiscite. One mark of Palau's new powers of self-government was that the responsibility for fixing the date for the plebiscite on the Compact of Free Association and the related agreements rested with Palauan President Haruo Remeliik. After discussions with representatives of the United States, President Remeliik first proposed that the plebiscite be held on November 5, 1982. Several people urged him to allow more time for the voter-education program, so he moved the date back to December 10, 1982. The president and vice-president of the United Nations Trusteeship Council, however, informed President Remeliik that even this date did not allow enough time for the voter-education program. On December 10, 1982, the OEK adopted House Joint Resolution No. 1–0099–8 setting February 10, 1983, as the plebiscite date. On December

16 Remeliik confirmed that the plebiscite would be held on February 10. This date would allow about three months from the first announcement of the plebiscite to the holding of the vote. President Remeliik felt this period was adequate for the political education program and the campaign.

The opponents of the compact, however, sought a further delay, in the hope that they would be able to make a strong enough campaign to overcome what they perceived to be the compact's head start. On January 11, 1983, Senator Moses Uludong introduced in the Senate a bill to defer the plebiscite to November 10, 1983. At about the same time the Senate Committee on Judiciary and Governmental Affairs declared that the voting date should be postponed so that the plebiscite would constitute a final and meaningful expression of the will of the Palauan people. The Senate adopted Senator Uludong's bill on February 1, but the House of Delegates adjourned *sine die* without taking action. Several non-Palauan antinuclear groups opposing the compact also petitioned the Trusteeship Council to delay the vote so as to enable non-Palauan opinion to be brought to bear. But the Trusteeship Council replied that fixing the date was the responsibility of the government of Palau and that they would not interfere. Thus the plebiscite was held, as President Remeliik had announced, on February 10.

This controversy, like the disagreements over the wording of the ballot and the fairness of the voter education program, was closely tied to the controversy over the merits of the compact itself. Most opponents of the compact and the related agreements, such as Senator Uludong, argued that three months was not enough time for the voters to understand the complexities of the long and legalistic compact. The compact's supporters replied that the basic issues had been discussed for well over a decade and that three months of intensive voter education and campaigning by supporters and opponents was more than enough to make the final vote a true expression of the will of the Palauan people. Some observers felt that the very controversy over the timing of the plebiscite drew substantial public attention to the forthcoming vote earlier than might otherwise have been the case and thus made a significant, if unintended, contribution to the voter education program. The same could be said of the controversy over the wording of the ballot.

The Wording of the Ballot. The wording of the ballot was much more complicated—and controversial—in Palau than in the other two jurisdictions. The complications arose mainly because, although as in the other jurisdictions the compact required approval by only a simple majority (50 percent plus one) of the voters, provisions in the Constitution of Palau required certain parts of the compact to be approved by three-quarters of the voters. These discrepant majorities played a major role in the campaign and outcome as well as in the wording of the ballot.

Section 314 of the proposed compact for Palau dealt with the future status of nuclear materials and weapons. It prohibited the use of Palauan territory for testing nuclear weapons and for storing toxic chemical and radioactive materials intended for weapons use. It also contained another, more controversial provision:

> The Government of the United States shall permit the presence of nuclear weapons in Palau only incident to transit and overflight, during a national emergency declared by the President of the United States, during a state of war declared by the Congress of the United States, in order to defend against an actual or impending armed attack on the United States or Palau, including a threat of such attack, or during a time of other military necessity as determined by the Government of the United States.

This section, unlike the other sections of the compact, could not be approved by a simple majority vote because of article 13, section 6, of the Constitution of Palau, which provided the following:

> Harmful substances such as nuclear, chemical, gas or biological weapons intended for use in warfare, nuclear power plants, and waste materials therefrom shall not be used, tested, stored, or disposed of within the territorial jurisdiction of Palau *without the express approval of three-fourths of the votes cast* in a referendum submitted on this specific question. (emphasis added)

In short, the rest of the compact could be approved by a simple majority of the voters, but section 314 would require approval by at least three-quarters of the voters. Thus it became necessary to put on the ballot not only the two standard questions (Do you approve of the compact? What other status would you prefer if the compact is not approved?) but also a third question asking whether the voters approved of section 314. It was agreed that the ballot would have three questions: question 1–A would ask whether the voter approved of the compact in general, question 1–B would ask whether the voter approved of section 314, and question 2 would ask the advice of the voter on what status should be sought if the compact were not approved. A major controversy soon developed, however, over the wording of question 1–B.

The original version of question 1–B, as agreed upon by the Palauan and U.S. negotiators in 1980, read: "Do you approve of the agreement concerning radioactive, chemical and biological materials concluded pursuant to section 314 of the Compact of Free Association?" After subsequent discussions, however, U.S. and Palauan negotiators decided to reword question 1–B as follows: "Do you approve the agreement under section 314 of the compact which places restrictions and conditions on the United States with respect to radioactive, chemical and biological materials?"

Palauan opponents of the compact, strongly supported by several non-Palauan antinuclear groups, protested the new wording vigorously on the ground that it spoke only of restrictions placed upon the United States. It did not mention that the essence of section 314 was its provision allowing the United States to use Palauan soil for the storage and transshipment of nuclear weapons and nuclear materials if in the judgment of the United States it was necessary to do so in a military emergency. Accordingly, on January 29, 1983, some anticompact leaders, headed by Senator Joshua Koshiba, filed a suit in the trial division of the Supreme Court of Palau asking for an injunction against holding the plebiscite on February 10, on the ground that the reworded proposition 1–B was misleading, created confusion, and inaccurately described the contents of section 314, which the voters were being asked to approve. The suit also charged that the Palauan translation of proposition 1–B was inaccurate, misleading, and internally inconsistent.

Two days later, on January 31, the court found that the revised version of proposition 1–B was misleading and in conflict with the law under which the plebiscite was to be held. The court ruled that the wording should revert to the original version, and that is what finally appeared on the ballot. Figure 2–1 shows how the final ballot looked.

The Political Education Program

Public Law No. 1–43, which prescribed the wording of the ballot and all other conditions and rules under which the plebiscite would be conducted, provided for the establishment of a political education committee consisting of five members appointed by the president with the concurrence of the presiding officers of the two houses of the OEK. On November 17, 1982, President Remeliik appointed, and the two presiding officers approved, Vice-President Alfonso Oiterong as the committee chairman and Father Felix Yaoch, S. J., William Tabelual, Lawrence Ierago, and Augusta Ramarui as members. Miss

FIGURE 2–1

OFFICIAL BALLOT
PLEBISCITE ON THE COMPACT OF FREE ASSOCIATION
FEBRUARY 10, 1983
REPUBLIC OF PALAU

PUT ANY MARK IN THE BOX INDICATING YOUR CHOICE ON BOTH
QUESTIONS OF PROPOSITION ONE AND ON PROPOSITION TWO.
YOU MUST VOTE FOR BOTH QUESTIONS (A) AND (B) UNDER
PROPOSITION ONE.

PROPOSITION ONE

THE COMPACT WILL BE APPROVED BY A MAJORITY OF THE VOTES
CAST

(A) Do you approve of Free Association as set forth in the Compact of Free
Association?

☐ YES
☐ NO

BEFORE THE COMPACT CAN TAKE EFFECT[,] SECTION 314 UNDER
QUESTION (B) BELOW MUST ALSO BE APPROVED BY AT LEAST
SEVENTY-FIVE PERCENT (75%) OF THE VOTES CAST.

(B) Do you approve of the Agreement concerning radioactive, chemical
biological materials concluded pursuant to Section 314 of the Compact of
Free Association?

☐ YES
☐ NO

PROPOSITION TWO

YOU MAY MARK A BOX BELOW TO INDICATE TO YOUR
GOVERNMENT YOUR PREFERENCE FOR THE POLITICAL STATUS TO
BE NEGOTIATED AND MUTUALLY AGREED BETWEEN PALAU AND
THE UNITED STATES IN THE EVENT FREE ASSOCIATION IS
REJECTED.

☐ A relationship with the United States closer than Free Association.

☐ Independence

30

Ramarui later resigned so that she would be free to campaign for the compact, but the other members remained throughout the political education campaign. The committee appointed Bonifacio Basilius as the director of the program, and he served as its chief administrative officer throughout. The United States provided $500,000 to defray the costs of the educational campaign, but the activities of that campaign were determined entirely by the committee and carried out under Basilius's direction.

The Political Education Committee (PEC) began by commissioning translations of the compact from the original English version into Palauan, Sonsorolese, and Tobian. Five hundred copies each of the English and Palauan versions were printed, and one hundred copies each of the Sonsorolese and Tobian versions were printed. These copies were distributed in the language preferred to anyone who requested them and were handed out at the various voter-education meetings conducted by the PEC.

The PEC prepared and published other documents summarizing the compact's main provisions, comparing the compact on several levels with the alternatives of independence, commonwealth, statehood, and the status quo. It also prepared and recorded radio and television programs. On the radio programs, which averaged fifteen minutes in length, members of the committee reviewed the compact title by title, explained its provisions, and answered questions asked by listeners. The committee also produced videotapes in which the committee members, the president, the vice-president, and the two OEK presiding officers explained the compact.

Television played only a minor role in the voter-education program and the campaign: under normal conditions television broadcasting is confined to Koror and Airai, and in December 1982 the television transmitter went off the air, to resume broadcasting only a few days before the plebiscite. Government facilities for recording and broadcasting were used not only by the government to present their voter-education program but also by Senator Moses Uludong, a leader of the anticompact forces, to present the case for a No vote.

The PEC also appointed a thirty-seven-member political education task force composed of representatives from each of the sixteen states. The members came to Koror for detailed instruction in the meaning of the compact's various provisions. The task force then divided into teams; the teams went to the various states and held at least three public meetings in each state. Each meeting was announced well in advance, and all citizens were invited and urged to attend, to hear the team's presentation of the compact's provisions, and to ask questions. At least once a week each team checked with

Basilius's office to get the answers to any questions it had been asked but could not answer to the citizens' satisfaction. Teams were also sent to hold meetings at places outside Palau where significant numbers of Palauans resided, including various parts of the Trust Territory, Guam, Hawaii, and California.

Several opponents of the compact complained during and after the campaign that the political education program was conducted too hastily and too superficially, that the indigenous-language translations of the compact were not accurate renderings of the English original, and that the program was so slanted in favor of the compact that it was propaganda rather than true education. Most observers, including AEI's scholars, did not agree. They were convinced that the program's administrators and education teams made a sincere and vigorous effort to be factual in their documents, radio and television broadcasts, and village meetings and that they provided accurate information for all citizens who sought it. The observers concluded, moreover, that there was no reason to suppose that the final vote was unfairly influenced by the program.

One general point about the voter-education programs in all three jurisdictions should be made here, however. In each case the same government that had negotiated and signed the compact also conducted the voter-education program. With hardly an exception, the officials who supervised the translations, prepared the documents and radio and television programs, trained the education teams, and conducted the village meetings supported the compact. No matter how conscientiously they performed their voter-education duties—and almost all of them were conscientious to the highest degree—there was bound to be a certain anomaly in their dual positions. The report of the UN observers of the Palau plebiscite sums up the problem—and its minimal practical consequences—very well:

> Some opponents of the compact alleged that the funds provided by the Administering Authority had been used for propaganda rather than education. . . . Such charges are perhaps inevitable when the programme of political education is established and to some extent conducted by a Government which has negotiated the agreement in question and is therefore committed to its support. . . . The Political Education Committee and the Director of the programme took seriously the injunction of impartiality, . . . but there were some occasions when the dividing line between education and advocacy may have become a little blurred. The Mission does not believe, however, that these seriously detracted from the effectiveness of the programme [and] it ob-

tained no concrete evidence to substantiate charges that political education funds had been improperly used to influence voters.[2]

The Campaign

In Palau, as in the Marshall Islands but not in the FSM, both the supporters and the opponents of the compact conducted highly visible and energetic public campaigns in the three months preceding the plebiscite. The campaign in Palau, however, was unique in that non-Palauan organizations played an important role in the campaign against the compact.

The Compact's Supporters. The forces supporting the compact were led mainly by the elected and appointed officials of the government who had negotiated the compact and believed that it represented the best post-trusteeship status for which Palau could reasonably hope. The most prominent figures for the compact were President Haruo Remeliik, Vice-President Alfonso Oiterong, Ambassador Lazarus H. Salii, and Carlos H. Salii, the speaker of the House of Delegates of the OEK. They did most of the speaking for the compact on the radio and television programs, and they and their associates organized the public meetings, parades, and other events making up the procompact campaign.

The Compact's Opponents. The forces opposing the compact were composed of two quite different groups of leaders and organizations. The first consisted of several native Palauan leaders, notably Senator Moses Uludong, Senator Joshua Koshiba, Senator Johnson Toribiong, and the Ibedul Yutaka Gibbons.

The second element of the anticompact forces consisted of a number of non-Palauan groups, some based in Japan, others in Australia, and still others in the United States, who opposed the compact mainly, although not exclusively, because of the nuclear provisions of section 314. The principal organizations in this category were the following:

The Micronesia Support Committee. This organization was headquartered in Honolulu, and its main contribution to the opposition's campaign was the publication of a sixty-eight-page pamphlet, "From Trusteeship to . . .?", which set forth the organization's view of the situation and the issues in all three jurisdictions holding plebiscites, arguing that the United States had administered the Trust Territory solely in its own economic and military interests, had corrupted Micronesian culture and made Micronesians dependent on U.S. handouts, and now planned to use the Compact of Free Association to make its domination permanent. The pamphlet strongly implied that the only honorable and viable future status for Palau and the other jurisdictions would be complete independence.

The U.S. Nuclear-Free Pacific Network. Based in San Francisco, this organization focused mainly on keeping all nuclear weapons, nuclear power, and nuclear wastes out of the Pacific. It produced several pamphlets and slide shows advocating that view, and its opposition to the compact concentrated almost entirely on section 314.

The Pacific Conference of Churches. This organization, based in Suva, Fiji, has as its members leaders of most of the Protestant churches in the area as well as the Conference of Catholic Bishops of the Pacific; in many respects it is similar to the National Council of Churches in the United States. It has generally opposed the presence of nuclear weapons in the Pacific and favored independence for the Pacific islands, and while there is no evidence that it played an active role in the campaign against the compact and section 314 in Palau, some materials generated by it were used in the campaign. Perhaps the most notable was a large poster declaring:

> If it is safe—
> DUMP IT IN TOKYO
> TEST IT IN PARIS
> STORE IT IN WASHINGTON
> BUT, KEEP MY PACIFIC NUCLEAR-FREE!

Focus on Micronesia Coalition. This organization, with headquarters in New York City, was a coalition of groups of church clergy and laity seeking to prevent the spread of nuclear weapons, wastes, and other materials in the Pacific. It too produced some anticompact pamphlets and posters circulated in Palau.

GENSUIKIN (an acronym for the Japan Congress against Atomic and Hydrogen Bombs). In the mid-1970s an organization was formed in Japan to protest and to stop the development and deployment of nuclear weapons. In 1980 the group split over whether it should condemn all nuclear weapons or whether it should exempt those developed and deployed by the Soviet Union. Those who believed that *all* nuclear weapons should be condemned reconstituted themselves into GENSUIKIN and cooperated with other antinuclear organizations in Palau and elsewhere in the campaign against the compact and section 314. Part of this effort included the sponsorship of an "education and solidarity conference" held in Guam in the week of November 17, 1982, attended by antinuclear activists from several places including Palau.

The Campaign against Nuclear Power. Based in Brisbane, Australia, this organization had the broadest program of all the outside groups working against the compact. The CANP opposed not only the compact in Palau but also the Marcos regime in the Philippines, Japan's alleged plans to dump nuclear wastes in the Pacific, the promotion of infant-feeding formulas in Pacific island societies, and the tour of the South African rugby team in Australia. It, too, supplied some pamphlets and posters opposing the compact, particularly section 314.

Many of these organizations participated in a 1975 conference that drew up a "People's Charter for a Nuclear Free Pacific." The charter was widely distributed during the campaign, and its main provisions make clear the grounds of their opposition to the compact:

We, being inhabitants of the Pacific, have agreed as follows:

Article 1: That a Pacific nuclear free zone be declared, including . . . all of Micronesia;

Article 2: That the peoples and governments of the Pacific will not permit any of the following activities or installations within this zone:

a. all tests of nuclear explosive devices including those described as "peaceful";
b. all nuclear weapon test facilities;
c. all tests of nuclear weapon delivery vehicles and systems;
d. all storage, transit, deployment or any other form of presence of nuclear weapons on land or aboard ships, submarines and aircraft within;
e. all bases carrying out command, control, communication, surveillance, navigation, and any other functions which aid the performance of a nuclear weapon delivery system;
f. all nuclear power reactors, excepting very low capacity experimental units, all nuclear powered satellites, surface and sub-surface vessels and all transit, storage, release or dumping of radioactive material;
g. uranium mining, processing and transport;

Article 3: that the peoples and the governments within the zone will withdraw from all mutual defense alliances with nuclear powers;

Article 4: that the peoples and governments signatory to this charter will work to ensure the withdrawal of colonial powers from the Pacific.[3]

The Positive Futures Center. Members of this Seattle-based group arrived in Palau at the beginning of February 1983 and remained throughout the plebiscite. A videotape they had prepared months earlier in Palau and elsewhere was shown repeatedly on Palauan television and in small discussion groups in Koror and Babelthuap. The film was highly critical of the Remeliik administration and its negotiators, but this aspect was removed when, under the title of "Strategic Trust," it was shown to viewers in the United States in May 1984 when the U.S. Congress was beginning its hearings on implementing the compact. Strong antinuclear, anticompact messages and attacks on U.S. policies during the trusteeship period dominated both versions of the film.

The Issues. Although many different aspects of the compact and related agreements were discussed during the campaign, three issues were clearly dominant.

First and foremost, once free association is established, should the United States be allowed to store and transship nuclear weapons and materials in Palauan territory? More succinctly, would section 314 be or not be an acceptable price to pay for free association? The compact's proponents argued that if the United States had this power it could defend Palau more effectively in time of war or other military emergency. They added that the United States felt it needed such a capability to defend itself and to maintain peace in the Pacific. Thus it was an entirely legitimate concession for the Americans to request. Moreover, the United States had no plans whatever to use Palauan soil to store nuclear weapons or to build a submarine base or any other major new military facility. Even if they had such plans, the compact would bring so many benefits to Palau that the concessions to the United States in section 314 against some highly unlikely possibility in the remote future were worth making.

The compact's opponents argued that the United States might well use its powers under section 314 to support and extend its aggressive and bellicose strategic policies and thus materially increase the danger of nuclear war in the Pacific. If such a war were to come and Palau were a storage center for American nuclear weapons, it would certainly become a prime military target for America's antagonists; and Palau might be destroyed in a war in which its own interests were not at stake. Even if nuclear weapons were never used and a war never came, the presence of such weapons on Palauan soil or in Palauan waters would pose major threats to the environment and to the health of Palauans. No benefit from relations with the United States, they said, would be worth such a cost.

36

The second major issue of the campaign was whether or not the United States should be allowed to use land areas in Babelthuap for bases and other military uses. (It was widely rumored, though often denied by U.S. officials, that the U.S. Navy intended to build a major new base for Trident nuclear-powered submarines.) The arguments of both sides were much the same as those made about section 314. The procompact forces said that such sites would probably never be used, but even if they were they would help the United States defend both itself *and* Palau better, that they would help preserve peace, and that they too were a reasonable concession to make to the United States in return for the compact's benefits to Palau. The anticompact groups argued that such sites would increase the danger of war and make Palau a military target in such a war and that the compact's benefits were not great enough to justify such risks. The procompact groups replied that the compact did not specify that military facilities will be built but merely preserves U.S. options to use Palauan areas if the need arises. There are, they said, no plans to exercise these options, and Ambassador Zeder had clarified the situation in his letter of November 1, 1982, to Palauan Ambassador Lazarus Salii; thus no such risks were involved.

The third major issue was whether the financial support promised to Palau by the United States was adequate or whether Palau could do better by achieving independence or by renegotiating the compact. The compact's proponents argued that the benefits promised by the United States had been arrived at after thirteen years of difficult negotiations, they were sufficient to support economic well-being and development in Palau, and, realistically speaking, they were the best deal Palau could hope to get. The compact's opponents declared that the proposed benefits were too small, they were guaranteed for too short a time, and they were not enough to justify the other sacrifices Palau would have to make.

So far as AEI's scholars could tell, none of the compact's Palauan opponents publicly advocated independence as an alternative status, and relatively few advocated commonwealth or statehood (although, in the election, 1,800 voters—24.8 percent of all voters—voted for independence and 2,250—31.0 percent—voted for closer relations with the United States). Their position seemed to be a "Yes-No" position—that is, Yes to the *principle* of free association, but No to this particular version of it, especially to section 314. If the compact were to lose, most of the opponents seemed to favor renegotiations that would eliminate section 314 and produce a new compact which they could support. The non-Palauan groups opposing the compact said little about what they would like to see in place of the compact; their prime object was to defeat section 314. Apparently the logical conclusion to be drawn from their allegations about the aggressive strategic and military posture of the United States, its record of colonial exploitation of Palau, and its lack of concern for Palau's interests was that the only proper post-trusteeship status for Palau would be complete independence—economic and military—from the United States. The plebisicite, however, turned mainly upon issues concerning whether this particular compact, section 314 and all, should govern Palau's future status.

Election Experience and Rules

Previous Election Experience. The 1983 referendum was far from being the first free and competitive election held in Palau. Prior to February 10, 1983, Palau had had elections for members of the Congress of Micronesia in 1965, in 1966, and in all even-numbered years from then until 1978—a total of eight elections in all. In addition, elections for members of the district legislature of Palau had been held in every odd-numbered year from 1947 to 1981, making an additional sixteen elections. Elections had been held for president, vice-president, and members of the OEK in 1979; and referendums had been held in 1975, 1976, 1978, and 1979. The 1978 and 1979 referendums were observed by teams of observers sent by the United Nations Trusteeship Council, and on both occasions their reports concluded that the conduct of the referendums had measured up well to the standards of free and honest elections. As a result, Palau began its preparations for the 1983 plebiscite with a well-established set of election procedures and a corps of experienced election administrators.

The Rules. The 1983 plebiscite was conducted under rules laid down by the OEK in Palau Public Law No. 1–43, which came into effect in November 1982. The law established as the main supervisory agency a three-member Plebiscite Commission to be appointed by the president. On November 30, 1982, President Remeliik appointed Sylvester Alonz, Daiziro Nakamura, and Emil Ramarui, and soon thereafter the members chose Nakamura as their chairman. The commission then appointed several persons, most of them schoolteachers, to serve as the local election officials presiding over registration and the casting of ballots. Collectively they constituted the Plebiscite Board, which was accountable to the commission. AEI's scholars observed an early activity of the board that illustrates the way the Palauans coped with their administrative problems. Two days before the election all the board members were brought to Koror for a final training and review session. Under the guidance of their supervisors they simulated all steps of the electoral process, from the original identification and certification of the voters through the casting of the ballots, depositing the ballots in the boxes, locking the boxes and securing them against tampering, and delivering the boxes for transportation to the central counting office in Koror. The session went on longer than anticipated, and Chairman Nakamura announced that he would have to adjourn it so the members would not miss the tide for making the return boat trips to their villages.

By law every citizen of Palau who was eighteen years of age or older on the day of the plebiscite was eligible to vote. The commission and board established several places for registering voters in the various states, and the deadline for registration was February 9, the day before the plebiscite.

Registered voters could cast their votes in one of three ways. One, they could vote in person on election day by going to the polling place in their home district, having their registration verified, and marking and depositing their ballots. Two, if they could not be present in their home districts on election day, they could vote in person at a polling place in another district so long as they were properly registered in their home district. Most of the voters in this category voted in Koror on election day; their ballots were put in special boxes marked with the names of their home states, and were later added to the boxes coming from those states so that the ballots of all voters from each state would be counted together. Third, if they were too ill to go to a polling place or were unavoidably absent from Palau on election day, they could apply, in person or by mail, for an absentee ballot, sign an affidavit stating that they were properly qualified to vote, mark the ballot, and mail it to the Plebiscite Board in Koror in an envelope that was postmarked no later than February 10. A significant number of votes were cast by absentee voters and by persons voting in districts other than the ones in which they were registered.

The commission established forty-two polling places in Palau and an additional special polling place in Koror High School for voters who were registered in other districts but present in Koror on election day. They also established polling places for students and other Palauans resident in Guam, Saipan, Yap, Truk, Ponape, Majuro, Honolulu, Fresno (California), and Denver (Colorado). They appointed at least two board members to supervise and manage each polling place in Palau, and the polls there opened at 7:00 a.m. and closed at 7:00 p.m.

The commission allowed each of three "sides"—the group that had supported the compact, the group that had opposed it, and the group that had taken no public position—to send two poll watchers to each polling place.

All ballots except those cast in Sonsorol and Tobi (where the votes were counted locally) were delivered in locked boxes to the central counting location in the Senate chamber in Koror. The commission appointed a five-member Counting and Tabulating Committee to count the ballots (one acting as caller, another as observer, and three as tabulators) by a time-honored procedure. The calls were made using a microphone and loudspeaker system so that persons outside the immediate counting area could see and hear everything that took place. The three scholars from AEI and seven observers from the United Nations were given privileged observation positions within the counting station and permitted to move about freely to observe all aspects of the count. Several observers and newsmen tallied the votes as they were called and discovered no errors.

The count began at 9:00 p.m. as scheduled. The ballot boxes that had been returned were placed against one wall. All ballot boxes bore numbers and were processed in a geographical sequence, beginning with Kayangel at the northernmost tip of the islands, so that observers would have a clear understanding of the source of the votes.

One team unlocked each ballot box and verified the contents by separating the ballots from the remainder of the materials. Then the ballots were given to the caller who called the votes on each ballot by question. Each of three committee members tallied the votes and upon completing the box verified the tally. As one box was being called and tallied, a second box was being emptied and its contents verified.

If, during the count, there was any question about how a ballot should be counted, the ballot was immediately examined and adjudicated by the committee members. In most instances, however, there was little question about whether the ballot should be counted. Only one ballot proved especially troublesome; it held up the count for more than fifteen minutes while the rules were studied and debated. The rules provided that any mark made in a box counted for that box and that more than one mark in the same box did not invalidate the ballot. The rules also provided that ballots should not be rejected for technical reasons if the voter's choice could be determined. In the instance of the troublesome ballot, the voter's choice was indicated by the letters "NO" in the YES box. After a lengthy discussion, the committee ruled the ballot invalid.

The counting, which began at 9:00 p.m. on Thursday, continued until after 4:00 a.m. on Friday. Unofficial vote totals from the distant and sparsely populated southwestern islands were obtained by radio and announced even though they were unofficial until counted in Koror. Actual delivery of these ballots took more than a day, and they were counted officially when they arrived. The ballot count resumed Friday morning after 11:00 a.m. and continued until 5:00 p.m., when a recess was declared to allow the United Nations observers to host a reception. The count resumed at 10:00 p.m. Friday, at which time a disputed ballot box from Guam was examined.

Two anticompact senators, Moses Uludong and Johnson Toribiong, filed a complaint against alleged irregularities occurring during the voting in Guam. They charged that there was no authority to conduct the plebiscite before February 10 and that the voting in Guam could not be considered absentee voting. They further charged that the affidavits completed by voters in Guam were notarized by Palauans who had no authority to notarize anything there. The two senators also complained that there was no written designation of polling places outside Palau, that the ballots cast in Guam were transported to Palau in a cardboard box, and that several unnamed persons who were ineligible to vote—because they had renounced their Palauan citizenship to become U.S. citizens—had cast ballots.

Voting in Guam and other places outside Palau was by absentee ballot. Mail delivery in Palau is dependent on air delivery, and only three flights per week go to Palau. To facilitate delivery of the ballots to and from persons who wished to vote at off-island locations, teams of election officials were dispatched to make available absentee ballots and return them to Palau before the deadline. To make this procedure as easy as possible, the officials designated times and places where absentee ballots could be obtained. These officials were also prepared to accept the marked absentee ballots, in their sealed dual envelopes, for delivery back to Palau. The sealed envelopes, which could have been deposited in the mail for delivery, were transported in cardboard boxes.

The Uludong-Toribiong suit asked the court to declare all ballots cast outside Palau void and to declare the plebiscite vote illegal and thus null and void. The court rejected the complaints against the procedures and accepted the administration's argument that they merely facilitated casting absentee ballots. The court also rejected the complaint that non-Palauans had voted because no specific individuals were named. The court added that ballots cast by Palauans overseas as well as all absentee ballots and others cast by affidavit were subject to challenge before being counted; even though the count took place publicly, no specific ballots cast by overseas Palauans were challenged. For these reasons, the court upheld the election's validity.

The total ballot count took several days, in part because the rules required that all ballot boxes were to be counted in the OEK building, one box at a time. The process of verifying the affidavits of all the persons who had voted at overseas locations or at polling places other than where they were registered also took a great deal of time. Moreover, absentee ballots postmarked no later than February 10 had to be counted if they were received in Koror no later than February 15. Thus February 15 was the earliest possible date the count could be completed. The whole process was lengthy and laborious.

When the count was finished, the counting committee reported its totals to the commission. The commission added the counts from Sonosorol and Tobi and from the overseas polling places and reported the grand totals to President Remeliik. The process was completed when the president officially certified the results to the OEK.

One unusual incident on plebiscite day is worth reporting since it involved a sudden change in the rules. As noted earlier, the instruction to the voters printed on the ballot said, "You must vote for both questions (A) [approval of the compact] and (B) [approval of section 314] under Proposition One." A separate set of instructions to the voters, however, indicated that their ballots would be valid and counted if only proposition 1–A were marked but would be invalid if only proposition 1–B were marked. They would also be invalid if only propostion 2 were marked.

Early on election day several observers called President Remeliik's attention to the confusion caused by these contradictory instructions. About 11:00 a.m. he ruled that any ballot would be valid and counted as long as the voter voted on at least one of the three questions. This information was transmitted to the team counting the ballots. It is uncertain, however, whether polling-place officials were aware of the change and whether they notified the voters. There had been no organized effort to encourage voting only on proposition 2, however, and apparently no voters actually voted only on proposition 2. So most observers thought that the change in rules, while irregular in its making and timing, had no apparent effect on the actual count or on the outcome. This last-minute change constituted the only substantial lapse in what was otherwise a well-conducted and fair election.

The Plebiscite Results

Turnout. According to the official results as certified by President Remeliik, there were 8,213 registered voters on election day. Of these, 7,246 persons voted. The turnout percentage was thus 88.2 percent, an impressive figure (well above most turnout figures in the United States) that continued the record of high turnouts characteristic of previous elections in Palau.

Votes by States. The votes cast in each of the states and other areas on the three propositions are shown in table 2–1. Obviously the most important facts listed in table 2–1 are those relating to the final result. In the voting on proposition 1–A the Compact of Free Association won with 4,452 votes Yes to 2,715 votes No, for a solid majority of 62.1 percent. The voting on proposition 1–B produced 3,717 votes in favor of section 314 to 3,309 votes against, and this favorable majority of 52.9 percent was far below the three-quarters majority required by the Palauan constitution. In the days immediately following the plebiscite there was considerable uncertainty about just where this ambiguous result left the compact. The Palauan Supreme Court, however, soon ruled that, since section 314 had failed to win the constitutionally required majority, the entire compact was defeated. We shall consider below where this ruling left the current and future status of Palau.

Table 2–1 also shows that a total of 7,167 voters voted on proposition 1–A and 7,026 voted on 1–B, so there was almost no dropoff between the two propositions, both of which had received a great deal of attention from the political education program and from all groups active in the campaign. Only 4,050 voters (slightly more than half of the total), however, expressed a preference for independence or closer relations with the United States in proposition 2.

From the comments made by active campaigners and ordinary voters before the plebiscite, one could discern three reasonably distinct positions: one was the "Yes-Yes" position, calling for a positive vote on both the compact and section 314; the second was the "No-No" position, calling for negative votes on both matters; and the third was the "Yes-No" position, which advocated Yes on the compact but No on section 314. The aggregate election returns listed in table 2–1 do not, of course, allow us to estimate the number of individuals holding these positions, but the state-by-state returns are suggestive. Of the fifteen states listed (the figures from Sonsorol, Tobi, and other outer islands were combined), eight (Aimeliik, Angaur, Kayangel, Ngeraard, Ngarchelong, Ngatpang, Peleliu, and the southern areas) voted Yes-Yes; six (Airai, Koror, Ngaremlengui, Ngardmau, Ngchesar, and Ngiwal) voted No-No; and only Melekeok voted Yes-No.

The crucial importance of the three-quarters requirement for section 314 is shown by the fact that while eight of the fifteen states

TABLE 2-1

RESULTS OF THE PALAU PLEBISCITE ON THE COMPACT OF FREE ASSOCIATION, 1983

Palauan State	Proposition 1-A			Proposition 1-B			Proposition 2		
	Yes	No	Yes(%)	Yes	No	Yes(%)	Closer Relationship	Independence	Blank
Aimeliik	128	63	67.0	116	73	61.4	48	36	111
Airai	56	164	25.4	52	166	23.9	39	128	55
Angaur	146	74	66.4	130	86	60.2	27	45	151
Kayangel	72	15	82.7	70	16	81.4	13	8	67
Koror	691	799	46.4	585	893	39.6	306	470	728
Melekeok	173	147	54.1	145	173	45.6	68	93	161
Ngeraard	208	137	60.3	179	161	52.6	71	85	192
Ngaremlengui	124	136	47.7	112	148	43.1	40	98	123
Ngarchelong	397	201	66.4	357	241	59.7	125	144	337
Ngardmau	72	95	43.1	57	98	36.8	29	54	88
Ngatpang	89	53	62.7	76	63	54.7	24	37	81
Ngchesar	101	115	46.8	88	126	41.1	42	88	87
Ngiwal	313	339	48.0	274	367	42.7	108	228	321
Peleliu	467	149	75.8	354	194	64.6	160	88	373
Sonsorol, Tobi, & other outer islands	87	3	96.7	84	6	93.3	58	3	29

Votes cast
outside Palau

Guam	517	72	87.8	408	170	70.6	457	48	89
Majuro	17	0	100.0	11	5	68.8	16	0	1
Ponape	51	8	86.4	23	36	39.0	46	6	7
Saipan	129	6	95.6	104	29	78.2	81	7	46
Truk	16	6	72.7	7	15	31.8	10	8	4
Yap	146	4	97.3	138	12	92.0	117	5	28
California	69	42	62.2	44	67	39.6	70	40	3
Colorado	62	12	83.8	57	17	77.0	54	17	3
Hawaii	161	35	82.1	120	74	61.9	121	35	40
Absentee by air mail	160	40	80.0	126	73	63.3	120	29	53
Palau total	4,452	2,715	62.1	3,717	3,309	52.9	2,250	1,800	3,178

SOURCE: *Report of the United Nations Visiting Mission to Observe the Plebiscite in Palau, Trust Territory of the Pacific Islands, February 1983* (United Nations Document T/1851, 1983), pp. 32–33.

45

voted Yes on proposition 1–B, only Kayangel and the southern areas gave it a majority of more than 75 percent; in the other pro-section 314 states the majorities ranged from 52.6 percent in Ngeraard to 61.4 percent in Aimeliik.

Another noteworthy pattern in the Palau voting is the relative closeness of the vote in so many states. In the FSM and the Marshall Islands, as we shall see, most voting districts voted either heavily Yes or heavily No—very few had small majorities one way or the other; and most observers are inclined to attribute this result to the strong influence of clan loyalties and the power of the traditional chiefs. But a strong vote for one side or the other did not occur in Palau. On proposition 1–A, the majority was more than 80 percent in only two states, in the seventies in two states, in the sixties in five states, and in the fifties in six states. On proposition 1–B, only two states were more than 80 percent, one was in the seventies, five were in the sixties, and seven were in the fifties. The frequency of relatively narrow majorities for one side or the other suggests that the clan structure and the power of the traditional chiefs is weaker on political matters in Palau than in the other two jurisdictions, but our data do not permit us to express more than a hunch about the situation. In any case, the frequency of narrow majorities was one major respect in which voting patterns in Palau were noticeably different from those in the FSM and the Marshall Islands.

A glance at the map of Palau suggests that the strongest opposition to the compact and section 314 came in the more densely populated and urbanized areas, especially Koror and the areas nearest to Koror, such as Airai, Ngaremlengui, Ngardmau, Ngchesar, and Ngiwal; and, conversely, the strongest support for the compact came in the less densely populated areas and those more distant from Koror.

As in the FSM and the Marshall Islands, there was substantially less voter interest in proposition 2 than in either part of proposition 1—quite possibly because the voters knew that their choices on proposition 1 would constitute binding decisions on important matters, while any preferences they expressed under proposition 2 would, at most, be advisory to future negotiations. In any event, of the 7,246 voters casting ballots, a total of 7,167 (98.9 percent) voted on proposition 1–A; 7,026 (97.0 percent) voted on proposition 1–B; but only 4,050 (55.9 percent) indicated a preference for independence or closer relations with the United States under proposition 2.

Of those expressing a preference, 2,250 (55.6 percent) marked "closer relationship with the U.S." and 1,800 (44.4 percent) marked "independence," a fact that may or may not be significant for future negotiations over Palau's status.

46

If one ranks the states according to their majorities on each of the three questions, it is clear that Yes votes on 1–A and 1–B are strongly correlated with abstentions on proposition 2—and with preferences by those who did vote for closer relations with the United States. Conversely, No votes on 1-A and 1-B are correlated with preferences for independence on proposition 2, although this correlation is weaker than the others. So it seems that most voters who wanted the compact were not very concerned about what status Palau should have if the compact lost, and many voters who did not want the compact preferred independence if there were to be no compact.

Differences between On-Palau and Off-Palau Voters. The differences in preferences between Palauans voting on Palau and Palauans voting in other areas are striking. Of the total of 7,246 votes, 5,682 (78.4 percent) were cast by persons living in Palau and 1,564 (21.6 percent) by persons living off Palau. As table 2–2 shows, the two groups voted quite differently.

The Palauans voting in other parts of Micronesia and in the United States supported the compact and section 314 much more strongly than did the Palauans voting on Palau. Also, many more of those voting off Palau expressed preferences for the options under proposition 2 than did those voting on Palau; and, by a wide margin (84.8 percent), they preferred closer relations with the United States, while those voting on Palau preferred, by a smaller margin (58.1 percent), independence. In the absence of survey data or other information about the preferences of particular individuals we cannot be

TABLE 2–2

ON-PALAU AND OFF-PALAU VOTERS IN THE 1983 PLEBISCITE
(percent)

Issue	Voters Voting on Palau	Voters Voting off Palau
The Compact		
Yes	55.6	85.5
No	44.4	14.5
Section 314		
Yes	48.8	67.6
No	51.2	32.4
Proposition 2		
Closer U.S. relations	41.9	84.8
Independence	58.1	15.2

SOURCE: Figures in table 2–1.

47

sure why the two groups voted so differently. It is worth noting, however, that nearly two-thirds of the off-island Palauans were living in Guam (a U.S. territory), Saipan (in the Northern Marianas), the Federated States of Micronesia, or the Marshall Islands—all areas that were already committed to close relations with the United States or were later to vote heavily in favor of the compact. It thus may be that the political climates in which they were living were more conducive to Yes votes than were their counterparts in the home islands.

The Fairness of the Plebiscite

The Palauan plebiscite of 1983 was short of perfection in several respects; yet, strange to say, some of the lapses seem to have improved the plebiscite's quality. For example, there was, as we have seen, much confusion and uncertainty in the early stages about both the timing of the vote and the wording of the ballot. The successive changes of date from the originally proposed November 5, 1982, to the final February 10, 1983, were confusing; yet the changes called attention to the plebiscite and gave the people an additional three months in which to acquire information about the issues. The sharp controversy and ultimate court decision about the wording of the ballot also caused confusion and uncertainty; yet that controversy too heightened public awareness of the significance of the choices to be made. We cannot say for certain, of course, but possibly both controversies contributed to the very high turnout in the elections.

On balance, AEI's scholars agreed with the observers sent by the United Nations Trusteeship Council that the political education program was as objective, factual, and fair as any such program can be, given the inevitable, if marginal, ambiguity arising from the fact that the program was carried out by the same government that conducted the negotiations, signed the compact, and brought the compact before the voters. Although some of the legal details were undoubtedly not well understood by many of the voters, the basic issues were thoroughly discussed in the voter-education program and in the campaign. Both the proponents and opponents of the campaign had full and free access to radio broadcasting and other means of communication and made full use of them. It seemed clear that many more Palauans listened to radio than watched television or read newspapers; radio facilities were freely available to all three "sides" on a first-come-first-served basis. In the ten days before the election, the radio station reserved ten hours each day for anyone wishing to broadcast comments on the compact. As far as we could tell, the compact's opponents were on the air more than its advocates, with

Senator Uludong speaking—sometimes live and sometimes by re-cording—more than anyone else.

The ambiguity over how many propositions a voter had to mark to cast a valid ballot was unfortunate, and President Remeliik's election-day ruling came after many voters had already voted; yet his ruling made casting a valid ballot easier, not harder. In other respects the casting and counting of the ballots was scrupulously accurate and fair, if laborious and inefficient. And, most important, our scholars, like the other outside observers, have no doubt that the final result was a fair and accurate expression of the will of the Palauan people on the three propositions put before them.

What was their will? In our view, the election results make the answer quite clear: A substantial majority of the people of Palau wanted the compact and preferred free association to independence, commonwealth, statehood, or any other alternative status. A smaller majority was willing to go along with the nuclear arrangements in section 314 if that was necessary to get the compact. A substantial minority, however, was not willing to accept section 314, and the three-quarters requirement of the Palauan constitution gave this minority the power to veto the desire of the majority for the compact—a power which it used effectively.

Postscript: The 1984 Plebiscite

After the compact failed to achieve the required approval in Palau in 1983, it was approved by the FSM and the Marshall Islands (see chapters 3 and 4), and in 1984 the United States began to fulfill its part of the bargain. President Reagan recommended to Congress that the compact be implemented for both the FSM and the Marshalls. The demands of the American presidential and congressional elections kept any final action from being taken, but it was clear that Palau had fallen behind the other two polities in the quest for post-trusteeship status.

The Palauan and American governments were both eager to close the gap, and so their representatives negotiated a revised compact, which was signed on May 23, 1984. It differed from the 1983 version mainly in that section 314 was deleted. There was no explicit reference to the storage or transshipment of nuclear materials. However, the United States took the position that a necessary consequence of its defense obligations and powers under the new compact would be the right to store and transship such materials when, in the judgment of the United States, it was necessary to maintain the area's security. Accordingly, the United States insisted that it would be necessary for the new compact to win the approval of three-quarters of the voters in a new plebiscite in order to satisfy the requirements of the Palauan constitution.

The plebiscite on the revised compact was held on September 4, 1984, with no UN observers or AEI scholars present. The only question on the ballot was whether the voters approved of free association as set forth in the revised compact, and the voters voted 66.9 percent Yes. That was still well under the 75-percent requirement, and so the revised compact also failed.

What, then, is the status of Palau after the two plebiscites? At the end of 1984 it was clearly different from the status of the FSM and the Marshall Islands; in both of those jurisdictions the voters had unambiguously approved the compact, and the U.S. government was in the process of implementing free association for both. (Technically speaking, all four Trust Territory jurisdictions—the Northern Marianas, Palau, the FSM, and the Marshall Islands—will remain Trust Territory districts until the trusteeship agreement is terminated for all four.) In early 1985, however, Palau's status was precisely what it had been before the vote of February 10, 1983: it was a district of the Trust Territory and would remain so until a new compact was negotiated, signed by both the government of Palau and the government of the United States, and approved by whatever majority or majorities are required by the constitution of Palau.

That approval may be difficult. The 1983 and 1984 plebiscites showed how difficult getting a three-quarters majority in a free and fair election is, and any future agreement that has to clear the three-quarters requirement is likely to be in similar difficulty. Whether the considerable ingenuity and good will they have shown in the past will enable the Palauan and U.S. negotiators to develop a new agreement that is satisfactory to both parties and capable of being approved by the voters of Palau remains to be seen.

Notes

1. For a more detailed discussion, see *Report of the United Nations Visiting Mission to Observe the Referendum in Palau, Trust Territory of the Pacific Islands, July 1979* (United Nations Document T/1813, 1980), pp. 7–11.

2. *Report of the United Nations Visiting Mission to Observe the Plebiscite in Palau, Trust Territory of the Pacific Islands, February 1983* (United Nations Document T/1851), p. 35.

3. Distributed by the Pacific Concerns Resource Center, P.O. Box 27692, Honolulu, Hawaii 96827.

The Federated States of Micronesia

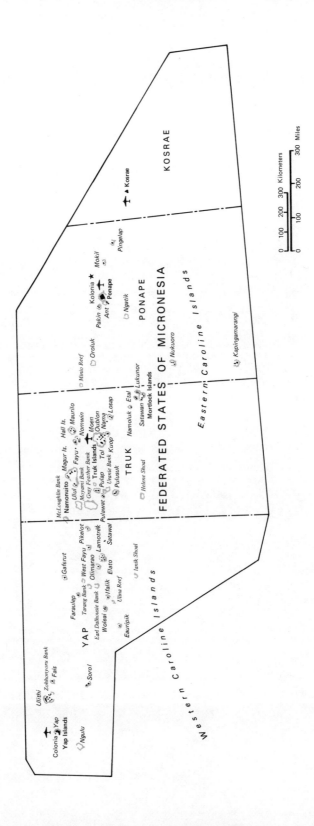

3

The Federated States of Micronesia

The circumstances of the plebiscite on the Compact of Free Association in the Federated States of Micronesia (FSM) were different from those in Palau and the Marshall Islands in several respects.

First, the FSM is substantially larger in both land and population than the other two jurisdictions. The FSM's total land mass is 689 square kilometers, compared with Palau's 492 and the Marshall Islands' 180. The FSM's total population is 73,200, compared with Palau's 12,100 and the Marshall Islands' 31,000. These differences in population were reflected in the allocation of representation in the original Congress of Micronesia (see chapter 1): in the Congress's House of Representatives, Truk had five members, Ponape four members, and Yap two members, for a total of eleven, compared with four for the Marshall Islands and three for Palau. If the proposed constitution voted on in the referendum of 1978 had been ratified by all three jurisdictions, the Truk-Ponape-Yap-Kosrae group would have had at least three-fifths of the seats in Congress and votes for president. This distribution of political power under the proposed constitution was perfectly clear to all concerned, and it was a major factor in the decisions of Palau and the Marshall Islands to reject the constitution and establish their own separate governments.

Second, linguistically and culturally the FSM is the most heterogeneous of the three jurisdictions. It has nine official languages as compared with four in Palau and two in the Marshall Islands. It is more diverse culturally and historically, and perhaps with regard to aspirations for the future, than Palau or the Marshall Islands. The most important of these differences are those generating the strongest separatist tendencies in the state of Ponape.

Ponape lies about 640 airline kilometers east and slightly south of Truk. Its main language is Ponapean, although it also has a small

51

enclave of Polynesians from the atoll of Kapingamarangi who speak Kapingi and have their own distinct culture. Ponapean is quite different from Trukese, the official language of Truk, and Ponapeans generally see themselves as being different from the Trukese in important ways. With a population of about 22,000, Ponape is larger than all of Palau, but it is still considerably smaller than Truk, which has a population of 37,500. During the periods of colonial rule by Spain and imperial Germany, Ponapeans resorted to armed rebellion far more frequently than Micronesians elsewhere. Their traditional desire for independence continues to manifest itself in Ponape's unease at being part of the FSM and in the ethnic Ponapeans' small majority against the compact and for independence in the 1983 plebiscite. Moreover, the traditional culture of Ponape, including the power of the chiefs, the *nanmwarki* and the *nankens,* has been less eroded by Christian missionaries and Western administrators than has the culture in most other parts of the FSM.[1]

Truk, Yap, and Kosrae are also quite distinct from one another, but their differences have so far not led to separatist sentiments as visible or as strong as those in Ponape, although there is a significant separatist movement in the Faichuk Islands in the state of Truk.

These wide variations in population and culture have several political consequences for the FSM. One result is the representation of the various states in the Congress of the FSM: Truk has six members, Ponape four members, Kosrae two members, and Yap two members. Consequently, in any policy conflict between Truk and Ponape, Truk needs the support of only one of the other two states to outvote Ponape, while Ponape needs the support of both Kosrae and Yap to outvote Truk. Moreover, since the president of the FSM is elected by the Congress from among its own members, Truk has a great advantage in the selection. Ponapeans are well aware that the first, and so far the only, president of the federation has been a Trukese, Tosiwo Nakayama, elected in 1979 and reelected in 1983. In the opinion of most observers, including AEI's scholars, President Nakayama is one of the most outstanding leaders in all of Micronesia and has made a considerable effort to be—and to be seen to be—the president of *all* persons and sections of the FSM rather than an advocate for narrow Trukese interests. Yet many Ponapeans think of themselves as permanently holding the number-two position in the federation; and even such concessions as locating the federal capital in Kolonia on Ponape and selecting a non-Trukese as vice-president (Petrus Tun of Yap in 1979 and Bailey Olter of Ponape in 1983) have not eliminated Ponapean separatism. Later we shall note the consequences of that separatism for voting patterns in the plebiscite.

52

The third difference from Palau and the Marshall Islands is that, even though in World War II Truk was one of Japan's most important military bases outside the home islands, today the FSM has considerably less short-term military significance for the United States than either of the other two polities. The United States has only a few minor military installations in the FSM, nothing remotely comparable to the Kwajalein Missile Range in the Marshall Islands. It has never tested nuclear weapons in the FSM, as it did in some northern atolls of the Marshall Islands in the late 1940s and early 1950s. It has never made proposals to the FSM for acquiring sites for military installations or for storing and transshipping nuclear weapons and materials. In fact, the only substantial strategic interest the United States has in the FSM is "denial"—the commitment by the FSM that armed forces of other countries will not be permitted to enter its territories and waters without the permission of both the FSM and the United States.

That situation may well have contributed significantly to the fourth difference: there was much less contention about the compact in the FSM than in Palau or the Marshall Islands, the election campaign was considerably less active and visible, and the general political temperature in which the FSM's plebiscite was conducted was considerably lower than that in either Palau or the Marshall Islands. That is not to say that there was no significant disagreement about the compact; indeed, the voters in Ponape actually produced a small majority against the compact. Even so, the plebiscite stirred up considerably less visible fuss in the FSM than in the other jurisdictions.

AEI's scholars made two trips to the FSM. Eugene Lee and Austin Ranney made the first trip to Ponape and Truk on February 14–22, 1983. The main purpose of this trip was to observe and discuss the voter-education program. During their stay Lee and Ranney held discussions with President Tosiwo Nakayama; Andon Amaraich, the FSM's foreign secretary and chairman of its Commission on Future Status and Transition; Petrus Tun, the vice-president of the FSM and chairman of the Plebiscite Commission; Ihlen K. Joseph, director of the public education program; Tom Bryan, director of the FSM Information Office; Gregory Swartz, counsel to the FSM Commission on Future Status and Transition; Erhart Aten, governor of Truk; Kisande Sos, speaker of the Truk legislature; Iskia Sony, plebiscite commissioner for Truk; and Edward King, chief justice of the FSM.

The second trip was made on June 17–25, 1983, by Eugene Lee (Yap, Truk, and Ponape); Austin Ranney and Richard Smolka (Ponape); and Raymond Wolfinger (Truk and Ponape). During this trip the observers renewed discussions with most of the people seen in February and added discussions with Bailey Olter, successor to

Petrus Tun as vice-president of the FSM; John Mangefels, governor of Yap; Hilary Tacheliol, plebiscite commissioner for Yap; Cunes Gustaf, mayor of Dublon, Truk; Father Amando Samo, parish priest of Dublon; Mitaro Danis, senior land commissioner from Udot; Kintocky Joseph, Udot magistrate; Bethwel Henry, speaker of the FSM Congress; Resio Moses, governor of Ponape; Janet J. McCoy, high commissioner of the Trust Territory; and Brother Henry Schwalbenberg, S.J., an American clergyman who taught courses in the FSM and later in the Marshall Islands about the compact's provisions.

Lee and Wolfinger observed the election-day voting on Truk, while Ranney and Smolka observed it on Ponape. All four scholars assembled in Kolonia to observe the counting. As in the chapters on Palau and the Marshall Islands, most of the descriptions and analyses presented in this chapter are based upon the discussions in which the scholars participated and on the documentary materials they gathered.

Preliminaries to the Plebiscite

The Draft Compact and Agreements. The terms of the Compact of Free Association and related agreements were negotiated for the FSM by its Commission on Future Status and Transition, chaired by external affairs secretary Andon Amaraich, and for the United States by a team headed by Ambassador Fred Zeder, the personal representative of President Reagan for Micronesian negotiations. Although the negotiations took considerable time and several difficult problems had to be resolved, the two parties signed the compact and agreements on October 1, 1982. The announced terms produced much less public disagreement and dissension than their counterparts produced in Palau and the Marshall Islands. This was due mostly to the fact that the documents' terms contained no provisions, such as section 314 for Palau or section 177 for the Marshall Islands, that aroused strong, vocal opposition from any organized or visible segment of the FSM's population or leaders. The proposed compact did renew attention to the concern in Ponape about its future relations with the FSM and in the Faichuks about their future relations with Truk and with the FSM, but none of these concerns were objections to the compact as such. In addition, the FSM's negotiators took special pains after each negotiating session to discuss the status of the negotiations with the FSM's traditional chiefs as well as with its top elected officials.

The Timing of the Plebiscite. The FSM and U.S. negotiators origi-

Eugene Lee and Austin Ranney with Ihlen K. Joseph, director of the FSM Voter Education Program. Joseph was one of many Micronesian election officials interviewed by the AEI scholars.

 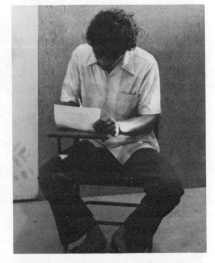

Above left: Polling place official, Kapingi area, Kolonia, Ponape. The polling place in this area was one of the community houses, and the voters marked their ballots on its floor. Above right: Typically voters in the FSM marked their ballots on desk-arm schoolroom chairs in a corner of the polling place.

Above left: Tallying Votes, Election Night, Ponape. Typically, two scrutineers read each ballot and called out its choices. The choices were then tallied on chalk boards. The whole process took place in the presence of many observers. Above right: Some voters used the exterior walls of the polling places as voting "booths." Yet no one tried to spy on how the voters had voted.

Sorting ballots, Election Night, Ponape. The first step in counting the ballots was to open a ballot box and sort the ballots and affidavits according to whether the voters were voting in their home polling districts or in districts other than those in which they were registered.

nally agreed upon June 14, 1983, as the date for the plebiscite. The United Nations Trusteeship Council, however, asked that the plebiscite be delayed a week to avoid scheduling conflicts for their team of observers, and the FSM, with the approval of the United States, agreed to set June 21 as the date.

In April 1983 the legislature of the state of Ponape requested that the plebiscite be postponed until January 1984. Their resolution stated that more time was needed to continue the public information program and to complete the subsidiary fiscal procedures agreement. This resolution was less clearly an anticompact ploy than were the comparable efforts to delay the voting in Palau and the Marshall Islands (see chapters 2 and 4), and it did not succeed. After consulting with the Plebiscite Commission, President Nakayama declared that such a postponement would not be in the best interests of the FSM and reaffirmed that the plebiscite would be held on June 21, 1983, as planned. In his response to the Ponape legislature, the president noted that all of the public information programs would be completed before June 21 and that the fiscal agreements were nearly completed. He added that it would be highly desirable if the compact were submitted to the U.S. Congress by August 1983 so that Congress could act on it before the distractions of the 1984 U.S. presidential and congressional elections.

Although not publicly stated, another reason for the Ponape legislature's objection to such an early date was concern about "election overkill," stemming from the many recent elections held in the FSM: in 1983 there were elections for the FSM Congress, a primary and a runoff election for governor of Ponape, elections for delegates to Ponape's constitutional convention, and municipal elections in many localities. Some feared that the voters might grow weary of elections and stay home on plebiscite voting day. But President Nakayama judged that delaying the vote further would do more harm than good, and the election was held as scheduled on June 21.

The Wording of the Ballot. Since the FSM Constitution has no extraordinary-majority requirement comparable to that in Palau, there was little controversy about the wording of the ballot. Clearly there had to be a Yes-or-No vote on the compact and its related agreements as negotiated; and clearly there had to be an advisory vote on what status the voters would prefer if the compact were defeated. Consequently the final ballot read as indicated in figure 3–1.

This ballot was quite straightforward, and, while the interpreting, counting, and tallying of answers to part 2 was, as we shall see,

FIGURE 3–1

OFFICIAL BALLOT, PLEBISCITE ON FUTURE POLITICAL STATUS
FEDERATED STATES OF MICRONESIA, 1983

PART ONE

TO VOTE ON THE QUESTION OF FREE ASSOCIATION WITH THE
UNITED STATES, PUT AN "X" OR OTHER MARK IN ONE OF THE
TWO BOXES.

DO YOU APPROVE THE COMPACT OF FREE ASSOCIATION AND
RELATED AGREEMENTS?

YES ☐   NO ☐

PART TWO

IN CASE THE COMPACT OF FREE ASSOCIATION IS NOT APPROVED,
THE FEDERATED STATES OF MICRONESIA AND THE UNITED STATES
WILL NEGOTIATE TO REACH MUTUAL AGREEMENT ON ANOTHER
FUTURE POLITICAL STATUS. YOU MAY INDICATE YOUR
PREFERENCE FOR A FUTURE POLITICAL STATUS OTHER THAN
FREE ASSOCIATION BY PUTTING AN "X" OR OTHER MARK IN ONE
OF THE BOXES BELOW.

☐ INDEPENDENCE

☐ A RELATIONSHIP WITH THE UNITED STATES AFTER THE
TRUSTEESHIP ENDS, OTHER THAN FREE ASSOCIATION.

YOU MAY DESCRIBE THAT RELATIONSHIP:

....
....
....

laborious, no one complained that the wording of the ballot was
ambiguous or that it was unclear what questions the voter had to
mark to cast a valid ballot.

The Public Information Program

Administration and Funding. On October 28, 1982, the Congress of
the FSM adopted an act providing that both the public information
program and the voting would be supervised by a plebiscite commission. The commission would consist of five members, one to be appointed by the governor of each of the four states and one to be
appointed by the president of the federation. The members ap-

pointed were Moses Mackweiung (Kosrae); Strik Yoma, later replaced by Delson Ehmes (Ponape); Iskia Sony (Truk); Hilary Tacheliol (Yap); and Petrus Tun (appointed by the president). Tun was selected by the others to serve as chairman of the commission.

The FSM Congress directed the commission to plan and coordinate the public information program; to plan, supervise, and administer registration and voting; to deal with any complaints about the fairness of the public information program or the voting; and to report the official results to the president of the federation for transmittal to the states and to the Congress for ratification.

At its first meeting, the commission appointed one of the federation's most able young civil servants, Ihlen K. Joseph of Ponape, to organize and administer the public information program.

The U.S. government agreed to provide $1 million to the FSM to conduct the public information program and the plebiscite. The commission decided that approximately half of this sum would be allocated to the four states and half would be retained by the commission. The special problems arising from the dispersion of so few people over such vast expanses of ocean are well illustrated by the costs of sending the public information teams to the outlying islands. In the state of Truk, for example, the cost of sending the teams on the motor ship *Micro Trader* to the Upper and Lower Mortlock Islands, which lie the better part of 320 kilometers southeast of the capital of Moen, was $2,150 per day for five days. A much smaller boat, M/S *Kokotu*, was used for 188 days at $200 per day, plus eighteen drums of diesel fuel. In addition, each member of the team had a per diem allowance, and the teams needed to take along supplies such as books, teaching materials, gasoline and kerosene, flashlights, batteries, and foodstuffs. The program was expensive; but most people, including AEI's scholars, felt that it was necessary and that the money was appropriately spent.

Translations of the Compact. The English version of the compact and related agreements is 275 pages long and contains both general principles and detailed legal statements on such complicated subjects as finance and taxation, international security, marine sovereignty, citizenship, and telecommunications (see the detailed summary in chapter 2). Translating it into each of the eight indigenous languages— Trukese, Yapese, Ponapean, Kosraean, Ulithian, Wolian, Kapingi, and Nukuoran—was not only the most expensive single activity undertaken by the public information program, it was also the most ambitious translation project ever conducted in Micronesia with the exception of translations of the Bible and of the 1978 constitution. Indeed, the published translations of the compact nearly doubled the total amount of material published in the indigenous languages.

The public information program employed several people, mostly schoolteachers, who were fluent in both English and one of the indigenous languages. Each translating team reviewed the English version line by line and translated it into the indigenous language, frequently debating the proper local equivalent for an English word or phrase. They often paused to translate the indigenous-language version of a sentence or a paragraph or a section back into English and compared the reverse translation with the original English version to verify the accuracy of their original translation.

The project unavoidably took many weeks. Was it worth the effort and expense? From one point of view it was not: only a few hundred persons gave more than the most casual attention to the translated documents; indeed, only 200 copies each were printed in the two least-spoken languages, Kapingi and Nukuoran. From another point of view, however, the project was well worthwhile: the very existence of the eight printed translations showed clearly that the compact was a Micronesian as well as an American agreement and that it was available to *all* citizens of the FSM whether or not they could read English. Even if only a few persons availed themselves of the opportunity, it had to be there, and was there, for everyone.

Activities in the States. In each of the FSM's four states, central coordinators were appointed to plan and administer the information program. Although the organization differed in detail from one state to another, the overall pattern was much the same. In Truk, for example, five major activities were carried on: task-force community visits, radio programs and interviews, community participation programs, training programs, and information activities relating to the plebiscite itself.

Radio broadcasts were used wherever possible. They involved live broadcasts of task-force meetings, which were also taped and edited for future use; statements by President Nakayama and Secretary Amaraich; and interviews with members of Congress and local leaders familiar with the compact.

Where the equipment was available, some of these activities were also videotaped and broadcast or played on videocassette machines. For example, a community television station that serves approximately half of Yap island repeatedly broadcast taped speeches and interviews about the compact. In Moen, the capital of Truk, there is no television station, but about 100 persons have videocassette machines. These were used for occasional neighborhood gatherings and provided a basis for additional discussion of the compact.

Especially noteworthy was a statement videotaped by President Reagan, in which he expressed his strong support for the compact and his willingness to present it favorably to the U.S. Congress if the people of the FSM approved it in the plebiscite. This tape was shown repeatedly on Yap television, and the audio portion was widely broadcast elsewhere. It was also the sole public presentation by any U.S. official during the public information program.

As one would expect in a culture that has traditionally relied mainly on oral communications and has made little use of written communications, printed material was much less important than radio and television broadcasts. The biweekly *National Union*, the official newspaper of the FSM, printed in English, regularly carried news of official statements and actions of the Plebiscite Commission and the Commission on Future Status and Transition concerning the forthcoming election but had little commentary on the compact's contents. In Yap, Governor Mangefels initiated a bilingual newspaper in April 1983 with the title *Mogethin/What's Up?* which carried commentary about the compact along with other public notices. Comparable unofficial newsletters were available in Ponape and Truk, but the combined impact of the print media was far smaller than that of radio, television, and, above all, personal conversations.

The Micronesia Seminar. In addition to the government-conducted public information program, a major education effort was mounted by the Catholic Church diocese of the Caroline and Marshall Islands, with headquarters in Truk. The diocese established an agency called the Micronesia Seminar, made it responsible for pastoral and social research in the area, and named Francis X. Hezel, S.J., as its director. The seminar employed Brother Henry M. Schwalbenberg, S.J., to prepare a series of memorandums on various aspects of the compact, including issues relating to Palau and the Marshall Islands, some of which were subsequently published in *Pacific Magazine* and the *Journal of Pacific History*. The seminar also permitted Brother Henry to assist various government voter-education programs when requested, and he presented a full-length course on the compact at the Community College of Micronesia in Ponape. This course resulted in detailed class notes that were duplicated for distribution throughout Micronesia.

The memorandums and class notes constituted the only major analysis of the compact made outside the government's public information program. Brother Henry's analysis was widely praised by several observers, including those from the United Nations, as complete, objective, factual, fair, and instructive. Its general tone is illustrated by the following excerpts of the short summary prepared and distributed by Brother Henry and reproduced as an annex to the report of the United Nations observers:[2]

Summary of the Compact of Free Association Made by
Brother Henry Schwalbenberg

I. The compact is about three things:
   a. Political—The Micronesian people, acting through their own constitutional governments, are self-governing.
   b. Economic—In recognition of their special relationship and to assist in efforts for economic self-sufficiency, the United States will provide the bulk of *money* Micronesia needs for the next 15 years.
   c. Military—the United States has *full* authority and responsibility for security and defense matters in Micronesia.

II. Military
   a. The United States has *full* authority and responsibility for defense and security matters in Micronesia which includes:

Rights	*Duty*
(i) Denial (until mutually terminated)	(i) Defend Micronesia (until mutually terminated)
(ii) Bases, no real bases in the FSM except the Coast Guard station in Yap (10 years) and civic action teams in the four states (15 years)	
(iii) Access, which includes the transit and storage of nuclear weapons through and in Micronesian air, sea, and land. Since the United States has no "real" bases in the FSM it has no place to store nuclear weapons even though it has the legal right.	

b. Micronesia cannot interfere with this authority, although there are some safeguards such as environmental standards, some restrictions on nuclear weapons, and the right to appeal directly and personally to the U.S. Secretary of Defense and/or the U.S. Secretary of State for a change of U.S. policy.

III. Economic
   a. The Federated States of Micronesia (population 76,050) will receive money over the next 15 years for the following categories:

	(Millions of U.S. dollars)	
General grants		755.00
Current	453.00	
Capital	302.00	
Specified grants		71.00
Energy	42.00	
Communications	15.00	
Civic action teams	14.00	
Block grants (social services)		105.00
Military impact payments (Coast Guard, Yap)		.16
Total		931.16

   b. The compact also provides for a few federal programs, primarily postal, weather, and disaster assistance.
   c. To help Micronesia become more self-reliant, the compact reduces the level of U.S. assistance over the 15 years. To make up for lower levels of money, the compact provides other ways for Micronesia to earn money, such as:
      (i) Local economic development, trade and tax benefits, money for infrastructure and development projects.
      (ii) Foreign affairs. The United States recognizes and supports the rights of the Micronesian governments to negotiate fishing agreements and other economic assistance from foreign countries like Japan and the United Kingdom.
      (iii) Immigration to the United States. Micronesians can go to the United States, look for jobs, and stay as long as they want. They will probably send part of their salaries back home to their families. Micronesians, if qualified, can also join the armed forces of the United States.

IV. Political
   a. The Micronesian governments operate under their own constitutions and run their own domestic affairs.

b. The Micronesian governments can also conduct their own foreign affairs, but they must tell the U.S. government what they are doing.
c. The Micronesian governments promise, under the compact, not to interfere with U.S. military authority.

Differences between Commonwealth, Free Association, and Independence

	Commonwealth	Free Association	Independence
Political	Micronesia has local government but is under the Constitution and many of the laws of the United States Micronesia is part of the United States forever.	Micronesia is self-governing under its own constitution, but cannot interfere with U.S. military authority. In the future, Micronesia could still choose independence or commonwealth.	Micronesia is self-governing under its own constitution. Micronesia would be on its own forever.
Economic	Micronesia becomes part of the U.S. economy, which probably means more money per person, federal programs, and better inflation adjustment.	The United States provides Micronesia with most of the money it needs to run its government and social services, and to start economic development projects.	Micronesia has to provide itself with most of its own money. The United States would probably give money for economic development projects but not much, if any, to run the government and social services.

Military	The United States has full defense authority, including the right to take land if needed. This lasts forever.	The United States has full defense authority but does not have the right to take land. Except for denial, all U.S. defense rights are limited to a definite time period.	Micronesia has to provide for its own defense, probably in the form of a mutual security treaty where the United States would defend Micronesia in exchange for denial rights for an indefinite time.

On the basis of work of this sort and with the support of the lay leaders of his church in Ponape, Brother Henry mounted an ambitious education program, supplementing the activities of the official public information program task forces. Starting with seven teachers who met with Andon Amaraich and other experts on the compact in April 1983, the group then made a presentation to fifty persons selected by the lay deacons of the several parishes on Ponape. This larger group went through its own training sessions, which concluded with an examination on the compact and a trial presentation before their fellow "students."

In May the group of fifty was divided into six teams, each of which visited an assigned group of villages on Ponape, spending two days in each place. The meetings, organized by the lay leaders of the parishes, combined social events and discussions concerning the compact. In general, Brother Henry felt that the effort was a success, a conclusion also reached by the AEI scholars and the UN observers. The UN report said the Micronesian Seminar "proved very useful [to the political information program]."[3] Brother Henry and his associates wanted to mount a similar effort in Truk, but it did not work out, mainly because the church's lay leadership there was not as strong as that in Ponape.

Evaluation of the Public Information Program. The public information program in the FSM faced problems similar to those experienced in Palau and the Marshall Islands: a great portion of the money and effort was invested in translating, printing, and distributing copies of the compact despite the fact that the society's traditions of oral rather than written communications meant that few copies were read in any detail; and the government, which had negotiated the compact and thus was bound to favor it, also conducted the public information program. Nevertheless, AEI's scholars concluded that the government's program was organized effectively, conducted conscientiously, and was generally factual, objective, and fair. Moreover, the Micronesian Seminar made a major contribution, especially valuable because it was conducted by private persons with no special axes to grind. All in all, public information in the FSM was even better than the comparable programs in Palau and the Marshall Islands.

The Campaign

Unlike Palau and the Marshall Islands, the FSM had no plebiscite campaign in the sense of Yes and No organizations making stump and radio speeches, distributing literature, putting up posters, holding rallies, or mounting any of the other activities we ordinarily think of as constituting campaigns. President Nakayama, Secretary Amaraich, and a few other leaders of the FSM government made some brief statements in favor of the compact, and Secretary Amaraich participated frequently in the public information program. But the procompact forces did not campaign in the usual sense of the word. A few opponents of the compact, notably Edwell H. Santos, the speaker of the Ponape state legislature, spoke critically of the compact in broadcasts on the government radio station. Otherwise there was almost no *public* pro-and-con discussion, and the political temperature prior to voting day was far lower than that in Palau and the Marshall Islands.

Yet the results, especially in Ponape, revealed that there was a good deal of opposition to the compact, even though few of the people who opposed it stated their views publicly and none formed an opposition organization. The results in Ponape considerably surprised most observers, including members of the national government; and they suggested that there had been, at least in Ponape, a good deal of private discussion of and opposition to the compact. Apparently several *nanmwarkis* and *nankens* in Ponape had quietly passed the word that the compact was not good for Ponape, and their followers voted accordingly.

The Issues. Apparently, also, several issues concerned the voters even though those issues surfaced in discussions in the public information program rather than in an organized Yes-or-No campaign.

64

From his participation in dozens of meetings on the compact in Ponape, Brother Henry concluded that town Ponapeans—the residents of Kolonia—were most concerned for the financial welfare of their families and especially for the future opportunities for their children. They wanted to know whether the levels of U.S. funding would change, whether Ponape's share of the funding would go up or down, and whether specific programs, such as Head Start and legal services, would be cut. Ponapeans living in the small rural communities outside Kolonia, such as Madolenihmw, Kitti, Net, and Uh, had different concerns. According to Brother Henry:

> Village Ponapeans . . . tended to concentrate on four not totally unrelated topics: a general and at times irrational fear of the military; the demeaning denial provisions of the compact; an almost anguished desire to keep the old ways; and a now-or-never hope for independence. Unlike the town dwellers, rural Ponapeans did not see U.S. financial assistance as supporting their way of life, but rather as eroding it. Also rural Ponapeans, perhaps naively, did not perceive an overwhelming economic dependence on the United States.[4]

Among older Micronesians, many of whom personally remembered that Truk had been the scene of a major battle in 1944, other concerns appeared to be especially strong: Will the U.S. military play a bigger role under the compact? Can we keep the big weapons out? Will the FSM become a battleground in some future U.S. war?

A third group of concerns important to many FSM voters had little to do with the language of the compact or its related agreements. These concerns stemmed rather from the internal separatist feelings and movements that are second only to economic development as the greatest problem facing the FSM. After all, the Federated States of Micronesia is striving not only for a new legal status but also for true nationhood and for the basic unity and loyalty among all its citizens that will make such nationhood possible when the FSM is no longer part of the Trust Territory. Because the Micronesians are divided by thousands of miles of open water, eight indigenous languages, several distinct cultures, and centuries of rule by four foreign nations with different institutions and attitudes, it is not surprising that regional loyalties loom large and Micronesian nationalism is tenuous. Moreover, the fact that three other parts of the Trust Territory—the Northern Marianas, Palau, and the Marshall Islands—have insisted upon and won separate status has made many people in parts of the FSM feel that they too should have and can probably get separate status from the federation.

These separationist tendencies are most important in Ponape. We commented earlier on Ponapean separatism, and we should add here that several persons in the FSM told AEI's scholars that the strong sentiment for Ponapean independence from the FSM plays a major role in all FSM politics. It was a considerable factor in the plebiscite voting even though it did not surface during the preelection public discussions of the compact. There is no question that many Ponapean leaders and citizens feared that the FSM would always be dominated by Truk; that the compact would, by giving more power to the FSM government, increase still further the power of Truk over Ponape; and that, as a result, Ponape would never be able to achieve its rightful place in the Pacific sun. Accordingly, it seems reasonable to surmise that many Ponapeans saw a vote against the compact as a way of sending a signal to Truk, the FSM government, and the United States that the prime concern of Ponapeans is that the identity and interests of their state should not be submerged any more than they already are.

In this nation of many islands, moreover, the pressures for autonomy are not confined to conflicts among the four states. The plebiscite was affected by another separatist movement, the longstanding attempt of the Faichuk Islands, which lie in Truk Lagoon within sight of the Trukese capital of Moen and contain about one-quarter of Truk's population, to become a separate state with a status equal to that of the existing four states.

The Faichuk story originates in traditional rivalries among clans and chiefs within Truk Lagoon. In recent times the issue has been manifested by the repeated requests of the leaders of the Faichuks to become a state separate from Truk. In 1982 this movement became so strong that it gained the support of the Truk legislature and, surprisingly, the FSM Congress; but it was vetoed by President Nakayama on the ground that there is a great need to build unity and nationhood among all parts of the FSM as a necessary precondition for establishing and maintaining true home rule. Separate status for the Faichuks, he said, would be a major setback for that objective. No serious effort was made to override President Nakayama's veto, but the issue was far from dead.

In the Faichuks as in Ponape, the compact became a surrogate for the quite different issue of local home rule—independence not so much from the United States as from the rest of Micronesia. At stake were the prerogatives of the traditional chiefs and magistrates, local patronage in jobs and public improvements, the ambitions of local legislators for higher office, and resentment against the Faichuks being ruled by decisions made in Moen. The strategy of the Faichuk

66

separatists, announced three days after the election, was to boycott the plebiscite altogether rather than to participate and vote No on the compact. And boycott they did. Turnout in the Faichucks was very light: of the islands' 6,218 registered voters, only 1,149 voted— impressive evidence of the influence of the Faichuks' traditional leaders.[5] The Faichuk boycott had a significant effect on depressing turnout in Truk and the whole FSM: if the Faichuks had voted at the same rate as the rest of Truk, the turnout in Truk would have risen from 49.7 percent to 59.0 percent. It also reminded all concerned that the FSM has yet to overcome many of its internal separatist tendencies and that building a nation after trusteeship has ended may well demand as much effort and leadership as ending trusteeship.

Election Experience and Rules

Previous Election Experience. Like Palau and the Marshall Islands, the FSM and its constituent states had considerable experience in conducting elections before the 1983 plebiscite. We have noted that Ponape, Truk, and Yap were all original districts of the Trust Territory and, as such, had elected members to the Congress of Micronesia in 1965, 1966, and in even-numbered years from then until 1978. All three districts had elected members of their local legislatures every two years since 1957 (Truk), 1958 (Ponape), 1959 (Yap), and 1977 (Kosrae). The four districts all participated in the 1978 referendum on the Micronesia-wide constitution; and, as the four districts that approved the constitution, they held their first elections for members of the FSM Congress on March 27, 1979. On March 8, 1983, less than four months before the plebiscite on the Compact of Free Association, the four states held their second round of elections for the FSM Congress. Consequently each of the states had a body of election laws and a corps of experienced election administrators, and it was relatively easy for the federal government to use this experience in establishing the rules and selecting the administrators for the 1983 plebiscite.

The Rules. On October 28, 1982, the FSM Congress adopted an act providing for the administration and supervision of all aspects of the 1983 plebiscite by the five-member Plebiscite Commission.

Although the plebiscite was conducted under rules laid down by the national government, the administration of those rules was largely left to the states. Each of the commissioners appointed by the governors of the states served as the plebiscite commissioner for his state (Moses Mackweiung for Kosrae, Delson Ehmes for Ponape, Iskia Sony for Truk, and Hilary Tacheliol for Yap). Each commissioner appointed several persons to supervise registration, preside over the polling places, and count the votes in the state; and the pattern of state administration of federal election laws characterized all parts of the election process.

Any citizen of the FSM who was eighteen years of age or older on the day of the plebiscite, who lived in a state of the FSM or, if living outside, considered the FSM to be a permanent home, and who was not mentally incompetent or serving a sentence or under parole for a felony was eligible to vote. Such persons could register to vote either before election day or on the day itself. Before election day they could file a brief affidavit, certified by two other registered voters and signed by an officer authorized to administer oaths. On election day a previously unregistered person could register at the polling place, and the requirement of swearing the affidavit before an official authorized to administer oaths was waived. Furthermore, for those previously unregistered citizens casting absentee votes, the regulations were amended to provide that an application for an absentee ballot could serve as an official registration form. The underlying idea, of course, was to ease registration to get the largest possible turnout in the plebiscite.

Voters could vote in one of three ways: in person at the polling place in the district where they were registered; in person at a polling station in a district where they were not registered; and by absentee ballot. Most persons voted the first way. They came to the polling place, signed opposite their names on the registration roll, and received a ballot. The voting place was typically a table or a schoolroom chair with a desk arm set at the far end of the room away from the election officials (although AEI's scholars did observe some voters using the exterior walls of the polling places as surfaces for marking their ballots). At first glance several outside observers were disturbed that such practices seemed to violate the requirements for guaranteeing the secrecy of the ballot; yet the observers soon realized that everyone at the polling places respected everyone else's privacy, and the voter's ballot was just as secret as if it had been marked in an enclosed booth. After marking their ballots, the voters deposited them in locked boxes, which were delivered to and opened at the central election headquarters in the state capital after the polls had closed. Special arrangements were made for people who voted in districts other than those in which they were registered. For example, many persons working in Moen have their permanent residences on other islands within Truk Lagoon. They were asked to vote at central polling places in Moen and to deposit their ballots in specially designated boxes bearing the names of their home islands. These ballots were then added to the ballots cast on those islands, and all were counted together.

Special polling places were also established in such off-island locations as Saipan, Koror, Guam, Ebeye, and Majuro in Micronesia, and Hilo and Honolulu in Hawaii. Separate ballot boxes for each of the four states were provided at each off-island location. Votes were cast two or three days before June 21, and the ballots were flown to the respective state capitals for inclusion in the count. Persons living off-island were also permitted to mail absentee ballots to the plebiscite commissioners of their states, but most chose to vote in person at the special polling places.

The scattering of voters among the many small dots of land separated by great expanses of ocean was even greater in the FSM than in Palau or the Marshall Islands, and the delivery and collection of ballots in these circumstances posed logistical problems unknown to most election officials in the world. For example, the ship delivering ballots to the polling places in the outer islands of Yap had to make stops at eighteen locations in a tour of several hundred miles. After the votes were cast, the ship reversed its course, stopped at each of the islands to pick up the ballot boxes, and brought them to Yap for counting—a journey that took more than ten days from beginning to end. The procedure was expensive as well as lengthy; but it was unavoidable, it was brought off smoothly, and it accomplished its purpose of giving every citizen of Yap a full opportunity to vote on the compact. Similar operations with similar costs and benefits took place in the other states.

Palau and the Marshall Islands are unitary polities, and in their plebiscites the votes cast in all localities were counted in the national capitals. The FSM is a federation, however; each state's plebiscite votes were counted in its local capital and the results were certified to the federal Plebiscite Commission by its plebiscite commissioner. In Kosrae, Ponape, and Yap the counting went smoothly. It started shortly after the polls closed and continued most of the night. In the presence of observers from outside, the ballot boxes were opened, the number of ballots cast and not cast were tallied and reconciled with the number of ballots originally delivered to each polling place. Two officials scrutinized each marked ballot and announced its choices to the tallying officials, who made the appropriate marks on their tally sheets. The process was made laborious by the need to interpret what each voter had done on part 2 of the ballot and to ensure that the vote was properly tallied. But the counters kept at it, and the final count was both fair and accurate.

In Truk, however, there were problems. The counting of the votes began in the legislature's building at 9:00 p.m. on June 21 and continued all night. The legislature, however, was due to convene the next morning, and so the ballot boxes had to be moved to the Public Affairs building. The process of tabulating and counting was slowed, and there was some confusion in the transfer of the boxes. At this point the United Nations observers remonstrated with the Trukese officials about the inefficiency and the risk of fraud and error, and the Trukese increased the number of counters and tabulators and handled the boxes more carefully. If the vote had been close in Truk these administrative lapses might have cast a shadow on the legitimacy of the count; however, the majority in favor of the compact was so large (95 percent) that none of the observers felt that the administrative bloopers invalidated the vote. Many did feel, however, that the decentralization of the count had its costs as well as its benefits.

The Plebiscite Results

Turnout by States. The turnout for the FSM and each of its states is shown in table 3–1. This table shows that the turnout rate for the entire FSM was 63.2 percent of the registered voters. This turnout was not only considerably lower than Palau's turnout of 88.1 percent (see chapter 2) and the Marshall Islands' turnout of 83.5 percent (see chapter 4), but it was lower than that in most elections in the FSM. For example, the turnout in the 1978 referendum on the FSM constitution was 76.5 percent, and the turnout in the elections for members of the FSM Congress held on March 8, 1983, only three months before the plebiscite, was 74.1 percent. And because, as we have seen, there had been so little public conflict over the compact in the months preceding the plebiscite, few observers were surprised that the turnout was this low.

The differences in turnout among the four states are also worth noting. Ponape had the highest rate of turnout, an impressive 79.7 percent, compared with 57.2 percent in Kosrae and 53.8 percent in Truk. Only Yap came close to Ponape, with 72.1 percent. Most observers concluded that the high turnout in Ponape and the relatively low turnouts in Truk and Kosrae resulted in part from the Faichuk boycott and in part, as shown by the results, strong opposition to the compact in Ponape and the weak opposition in the other states.

Votes on the Compact: The Overall Result. The votes in the FSM and in each of the states on both parts of the ballot are summarized in table 3–2. The most striking fact in table 3–2 is that the states of

70

TABLE 3–1

VOTER TURNOUT BY STATES,
FEDERATED STATES OF MICRONESIA PLEBISCITE AND ELECTIONS, 1983

State	Registered Voters[a]	Votes Cast in Plebiscite[b]	Plebiscite Voter Turnout (%)	Votes Cast in Elections	Election Voter Turnout (%)
Kosrae	2,628	1,503	57.2	1,732	65.9
Ponape	10,908	8,694	79.7	9,533	87.4
Truk	22,136	11,902	53.8	15,561	70.3
Yap	4,866	3,507	72.1	3,202	65.8
Total	40,538	25,606	63.2	30,048	74.1

a. The figures given for Truk and Yap include those persons who registered to vote on the day of the plebiscite; the Ponape and Kosrae figures are the pre-plebiscite registration totals.
b. The figures represent the votes cast on part 1 of the ballot.
SOURCE: *Report of the United Nations Visiting Mission to Observe the Plebiscite in the Federated States of Micronesia, Trust Territory of the Pacific Islands, June 1983* (United Nations Document T/1860, 1984), p. 16.

Kosrae, Truk, and Yap all voted overwhelmingly in favor of the compact, but the state of Ponape, by a narrow margin (51.1 percent), voted against it. The difference between Ponape and the other states is emphasized by the fact that on part 1 Ponape cast 4,437 of the total 5,348 No votes cast in the whole FSM—83.0 percent of the total. In the other three states the combined votes were 15,873 Yes to 911 No, a majority of 94.6 percent for the compact. So the difference between Ponape and the other states was one of the most striking features of the outcome, and the Ponape results merit closer attention.

Votes on the Compact: The Results in Ponape. Brother Henry Schwalbenberg's analysis suggests that the results in Ponape should be explained mainly in terms of a conflict between the ethnic Ponapeans living in the rural municipalities on the one hand and the residents of Kolonia, Sokehs, and the outer islands on the other. The returns from each of these areas are shown in table 3–3. The figures show strong Yes majorities in Kolonia, Sokehs, and the outer islands, and equally strong No majorities in Ponape's rural municipalities other than Sokehs. Added together, the rural areas cast 49 percent of the state's votes and had a collective No majority of 66 percent. Kolonia, Sokehs, and the outer islands cast 36 percent of the votes and had a collective Yes majority of 65 percent.

TABLE 3–2

VOTES BY STATES,
FEDERATED STATES OF MICRONESIA PLEBISCITE, 1983

| | Part 1 | | | | | Part 2 | | | |
State	Yes	No	% Yes	Independence	Total Other Relations with U.S.	Commonwealth	U.S. Territory	Statehood	Other, or no description
Kosrae	1,325	172	88.5	401	793	211	124	173	285
Ponape	4,248	4,437	48.9	4,767	2,004	821	424	278	481
Truk	11,261	538	95.4	7,252	1,655	96	92	38	1,429
Yap	3,287	201	94.2	1,504	732	191	180	79	392
Total	20,121	5,348	79.0	13,924	5,184	1,319	820	568	2,587

SOURCE: *Report of the United Nations Visiting Mission to Observe the Plebiscite in the Federated States of Micronesia, Trust Territory of the Pacific Islands, June 1983* (United Nations Document T/1860, 1984), pp. 14–15.

TABLE 3-3

VOTES BY MUNICIPALITY, STATE OF PONAPE, FEDERATED STATES OF MICRONESIA PLEBISCITE, 1983

	Total Votes Cast	Part 1 % Yes	Part 2: % Voting		
			Independence	Closer Ties to U.S.	Blank or Void
Kolonia	789	61.7	29.4	44.7	25.9
Rural Municipalities					
Sokehs	1,364	62.0	44.1	35.3	20.5
Madolenihmw	1,169	38.9	69.3	17.5	13.5
Kitti	1,153	31.8	75.8	8.9	15.4
Net	934	26.9	84.4	9.2	6.4
Uh	982	37.5	82.5	8.9	8.5
Outer Islands	948	70.7	16.9	65.2	17.8
Absentee					
On-island	1,191	56.5	37.8	37.8	24.4
Off-island	155	85.2	23.9	56.8	19.4
Total	8,685	48.9	54.8	28.5	16.7

SOURCE: Henry M. Schwalbenberg, S.J., "Independence and Unity or Money: The Plebiscite in the FSM," Micronesian Seminar Memorandum #10 (January 1984), table 2, p. 7.

Why these differences? Brother Henry makes a convincing case for the proposition that the compact split the people of Ponape along both economic and ethnic lines. Kolonia is Ponape's only town, the main site of its commerce, employment, and wealth, and the seat of the state and national governments. Its economic viability, like that of all Micronesian towns, rests almost entirely on U.S. grants to finance the state and national governments. Hence Kolonia voted strongly for the compact, and, on part 2, joined the outer islands as the only areas that preferred closer ties with the United States to independence as an alternative to the compact.

Also, much of Kolonia's population consists of non-Ponapeans from the outer islands of Kapingamarangi, Ngatik, Nukuoro, Oroluk, and Mokil who have migrated to Kolonia in search of better jobs. Like their relatives remaining on the outer islands (who voted 71 percent Yes), they supported the compact.

Economically the municipality of Sokehs is similar to Ponape's other rural areas, but ethnically it is not. The original Ponapean inhabitants of Sokehs rebelled against German rule in the early 1900s and were deported. The area was gradually repopulated mainly by immigrants from Truk's Mortlock Islands and Ponape's outer islands, and it remains ethnically non-Ponapean as well as rural. As Brother Henry noted, Secretary Andon Amaraich, the FSM's chief negotiator for the compact and one of its most effective advocates, is himself a Mortlockese and thus was able to speak directly in the Mortlock language to large gatherings in Sokehs before the plebiscite.

Brother Henry summed up the situation in Ponape thus:

> Local voting patterns seem symptomatic of the rapid social and economic change occurring in Ponape. Localized economic growth has led to a town-versus-village rift. The influx of non-ethnic Ponapeans to this town and on to high political positions in the national government has added a racial element to this growing estrangement. These tensions are only exacerbated . . . by the discord between the state and national leadership. . . . Since the early '70s traditional Ponapean leaders have been on record as opposing free association and favoring independence. These leaders perceive growing westernization as eroding the traditional foundations of their social prestige and influence. This position favoring independence by traditional ethnic Ponapean leaders may go some way in explaining the cohesiveness of the vote against the Compact among rural ethnic Ponapeans.[6]

Votes on the Alternatives. Table 3–2 shows that a heavier vote was cast in the FSM on the advisory question in part 2 than was cast in either Palau or the Marshall Islands: a total of 25,469 votes were cast on part 1, and 19,218 (75.5 percent as many) on part 2. This was far higher than the 56.5 who voted on the advisory question in Palau and higher still than the 29.3 percent who voted on it in the Marshall Islands. Perhaps the vote was heavy because there was no FSM counterpart of Palau's section 314 or the Marshall Islands' section 177 to divert attention from the question of what status the people wanted if the compact were rejected. After all, the people of the FSM were voting after the people of Palau, in effect, had rejected the compact, and the question of where that rejection left the Palauans' hopes for the future may well have been on the minds of the leaders and voters in the FSM.

In any case, table 3–4 shows the support given to the various alternatives in part 2 by the FSM's voters.

During the negotiations and the plebiscite campaign, the FSM's leaders, particularly President Nakayama and Secretary Amaraich, took the position that independence was the best alternative in part 2—partly because it was the most dignified and partly because, if the compact were rejected, a large vote for independence would

TABLE 3–4

VOTES BY STATES ON PART 2, FEDERATED STATES OF MICRONESIA PLEBISCITE, 1983

Alternative Status Preferred	Kosrae	Ponape	Truk	Yap	FSM Totals	%[a]
Independence	401	4,767	7,252	1,504	13,924	72.5
Commonwealth	211	821	96	191	1,319	6.9
U.S. territory	124	424	92	180	820	4.3
Statehood	173	278	38	79	568	3.0
Other, no description	285	481	1,429	392	2,587	13.5
Total	1,194	6,771	.8,907	2,346	19,218	100.2

a. Details do not add to 100% because of rounding.
SOURCE: The figures in table 3–2.

strengthen the position of the FSM in future negotiations with the United States. The figures in table 3–4 show that most Micronesians agreed with President Nakayama's statement after the voting that "on Part Two of the Ballot, 'Independence' was chosen by the FSM voters as the only viable alternative."[7] Of the 19,218 who voted on part 2, 13,924 (72.5 percent) marked their preference for independence if the compact were defeated. Another 2,587 (13.4 percent) marked "other relationship" but did not describe which one they preferred. And the remainder scattered their preferences among commonwealth status (6.9 percent), U.S. territorial status (4.3 percent), and U.S. statehood (2.9 percent).

Three of the four states strongly supported the independence alternative. Its majority over the other choices, not including the "other, no description" choice, was 97 percent in Truk, 77 percent in Yap, and 76 percent in Ponape. In Kosrae independence was supported by only 44 percent, and the majority preferred a closer relationship to the United States if the compact lost.

The voting on part 2 shed considerable light on how the Micronesians feel about their future, but the overriding fact emerging from the plebiscite was that the great majority of the people in Kosrae, Truk, and Yap, but not in Ponape, approved the Compact of Free Association as the best available basis for that future.

The Fairness of the Plebiscite

The FSM's conduct of the public information program and the voting had a few lapses. The low attendance at the public information program's local meetings was disappointing, although perhaps inevitable given the lack of public controversy about the compact. But the educational materials were well prepared, the meetings were conducted with energy and objectivity, and they adhered scrupulously to the mandate to be objective and factual rather than to advocate Yes votes. Moreover, Brother Henry's seminar on the compact and his short summary of the compact's main provisions were substantial contributions to popular understanding. The absence of public controversy between the Yes and No forces made the issues less prominent than they might have been, and it would have been better if the considerable opposition in Ponape had been more publicly discussed rather than left largely to private conversations among individuals and between traditional chiefs and their followers. Yet, if the pro and con forces did not wish to make their cases publicly, there was no democratic way they could be forced to do so. Fairness in campaigning means an equal *opportunity* for all sides to be heard, and outside observers generally agreed that such opportunities were fully available in the FSM.

The boycott of the election in the Faichuks was unfortunate, but it was the choice of the area's leaders, and one can hardly see how it could have been prevented. Certainly no official of either the FSM government or the government of Truk tried to discourage voting in the Faichuks in any way; quite the opposite, in fact. The careless administration of the storage, movement, and counting of the ballots in Truk might have caused more concern if the vote there had been close; but no observer believed that Truk's lapses were due to anything but inefficiency or that they had a significant effect on the outcome.

Accordingly, AEI's scholars and the United Nations observers concluded that the FSM's public information program was fair to all points of view and that the final vote constituted an accurate expression of the will of the FSM's people—including the people of Ponape.

After the Plebiscite

The FSM constitution and the FSM Congress's act of October 28, 1982, stipulated that the compact would be considered approved by the FSM after the completion of three steps: approval by an FSM-wide majority of the voters in the June 21 plebiscite; approval by majorities of the legislatures in at least two-thirds (three out of four) of the states; and approval by a two-thirds majority (ten out of fourteen) of the members of the FSM's Congress.

In early July the Plebiscite Commission certified to President Nakayama the outcome of the plebiscite (as we have shown it in table

3–2). On July 13 the president officially notified the four state legislatures of the outcome and requested them to act on the compact as soon as possible.

Not surprisingly, each of the state legislatures then proceeded to vote as the state's voters had voted in the plebiscite. On July 29 the Truk legislature voted 21–1 to ratify the compact. On August 12 the Yap legislature voted unanimously to ratify. On August 17 the Kosrae legislature voted unanimously to ratify. And on September 2 the Ponape legislature voted 17–2 *not* to ratify.

During the ratification period there was some concern about whether the procompact forces would be able to muster the required two-thirds vote in the FSM Congress. After all, Ponape has four votes in the Congress, and if all four were to be cast against the compact—a not-unreasonable expectation in view of Ponape's negative majorities in both the plebiscite and the state legislature—then all of the other members would have to vote in favor of the compact, and an abstention or absence by just one would be enough to defeat the compact despite the overwhelming FSM-wide popular majority for it in the plebiscite.

In the event, those apprehensions turned out to be unjustified. On September 2, a short time after the Ponape legislature had voted, the FSM Congress voted unanimously to approve the compact. Senator Pedro Harris, who had been elected to the Congress from Ponape in the July 15 election, explained his vote to ratify the compact thus:

> The Compact represents to some of us in Ponape a first step toward self-determination, giving us the opportunity to seek and fulfill our values and beliefs. This is the "Yes" vote expressed in Ponape and the FSM.
>
> Those who vote "Yes" believe that from here we can iron out the differences with the United States, but most importantly, we are going to share that self-determination together as Yapese, Trukese, Ponapeans, and Kosraeans.
>
> Our legends tell us that we are one people; now we are given this opportunity to remake ourselves again as one people. This is the most valuable aspect of the Compact.
>
> As a representative of the State of Ponape that voted "No," and at the same time a lot of people voted "Yes," I cast my vote with those who voted "Yes," with a great deal of respect for those who voted "No."[8]

On September 8 President Nakayama sent a letter to President Reagan notifying him that the FSM had completed its ratification of the compact. It was the first of the three Trust Territory jurisdictions to do so. Now the United States had to fulfill its part of the bargain.

Notes

1. Francis X. Hezel, S.J., *The First Taint of Civilization* (Honolulu: University of Hawaii Press, 1983), pp. 109–70; and Francis X. Hezel, S.J., and M. L. Berg, eds., *Micronesia: Winds of Change* (Saipan: Trust Territory of the Pacific Islands, 1980), passim.

2. *Report of the United Nations Visiting Mission to Observe the Plebiscite in the Federated States of Micronesia, Trust Territory of the Pacific Islands, June 1983* (United Nations Document T/1860, 1984), pp. 27–30.

3. Ibid., p. 3.

4. Henry M. Schwalbenberg, S.J., "Independence and Unity or Money: The Plebiscite in the FSM," Micronesian Seminar Memorandum #10 (January 1984), p. 15.

5. Ibid., table 3, p. 19.

6. Ibid., pp. 9, 12.

7. *National Union* (July 15, 1983), p. 4.

8. *National Union* (September 15, 1983), p. 4.

The Marshall Islands

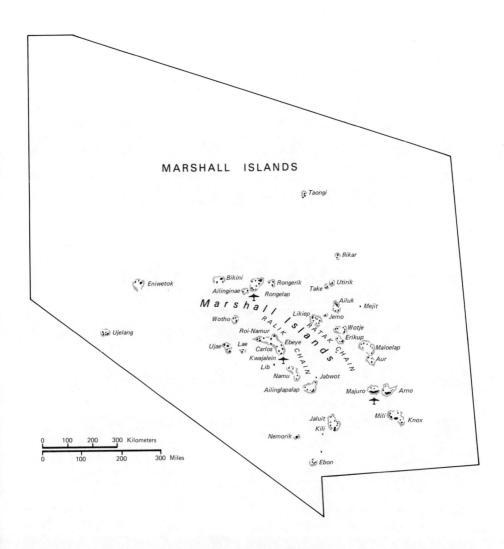

MARSHALL   ISLANDS

Taongi

Bikar

Eniwetok

Bikini

Rongerik   Utirik

Ailinginae   Rongelap   Take

Ailuk   Mejit

Likiep   Jemo

Wotho   Roi-Namur   Wotje

RALIK   Erikup

Ujelang   Ujae   Lae   Ebeye   Maloelap

Carlos   Aur

Kwajalein   CHAIN

Lib

Namu   Jabwot

Ailinglapalap   Majuro   Arno

Jaluit   Mili   Knox

Kili

Nemorik   Ebon

M a r s h a l l   I s l a n d s

RATAK CHAIN

0   100   200   300   Kilometers

0   100   200   300   Miles

4

The Marshall Islands

The last of the Micronesian plebiscites of 1983 was held in the Republic of the Marshall Islands (Repmar) on September 7. The compact was publicly disputed in the Marshalls at least as hotly as in Palau and a good deal more so than in the FSM. Moreover, in several respects the United States had a more obvious and important stake in the outcome in Repmar than in the other two jurisdictions.

First, the United States had only contingency plans for the possible use of Palauan territory for future military facilities, but it had already invested billions of dollars in the Marshall Islands in constructing and operating the Kwajalein Missile Range (KMR). The Department of Defense was therefore gravely concerned with any political development that might skyrocket the rental charges or perhaps even force the relocation of the facility.

Second, in the late 1940s and early 1950s the United States had tested several nuclear devices in some northern parts of the Marshall Islands, particularly on Bikini and Enewetak. In the course of these tests the residents of Bikini and Enewetak were relocated to other parts of the Marshalls, and residents of other islands in the vicinity, especially Rongelap and Utirik, were exposed to radioactive fallout from the nuclear detonations. (Some residents of other northern atolls, such as Ailuk, Lae, Likiep, Mejit, Wotho, and Wotje, felt that they too had been damaged by fallout, but to date the evidence is inconclusive.) The United States had already compensated the Marshallese adversely affected by the tests, but many private suits claiming further payments had been brought by Marshallese plaintiffs against the U.S. government in U.S. courts. These suits were being litigated, on a contingency fee basis, by Honolulu- and mainland-based lawyers representing the Marshallese claimants. These lawyers joined together in an organization called the Marshall Islands Atomic

Testing Litigation Project (MIATLP), and their claims totaled more than $4 billion. Thus it was in the interest of the United States to settle these claims permanently and for a reasonable figure.

These circumstances and the special problems of conducting plebiscites in Micronesian conditions made the plebiscite in the Marshall Islands especially interesting for AEI's scholars, who made three trips to the area. Austin Ranney and Raymond Wolfinger made the first trip on November 12–21, 1982. They arrived in Majuro on November 14, went from Majuro to Kwajalein on November 18, and returned from Majuro to the mainland on November 19–21. The primary purpose of this initial visit was to observe and discuss the voter-education program. During their stay on Majuro, Ranney and Wolfinger held discussions with Marshallese election officials and leaders of both the procompact and anticompact sides. Their most extensive discussions were held with Carmen Bigler, the director of the Political Education Commission; Shiro E. Riklon, Repmar's chief electoral officer; Dan Smith, editor of the *Marshall Islands Journal*; Kinja Andrike, head of the Department of Education; Gerald Knight, curator of the Alele Museum; George Allen, a leading attorney for the Kwajalein Atoll Corporation (KAC); Hermios Kibin, chief electoral officer for Kwajalein atoll; Father Hacker, pastor of the Roman Catholic Mission on the island of Ebeye in Kwajalein atoll; Carl Ingram, attorney general of Repmar; Colonel John Beavers, head of public relations for the KMR; Oscar de Brum, chief secretary (head of the civil service) for Repmar; and Amata Kabua, president of Repmar.

Richard Smolka made the second visit on August 8–14, 1983. This special visit was precipitated by the July 18 resignation of two anticompact members of the Political Education Commission, Jack Jorbon and Laninruj Abon. During his visit Smolka had extended discussions with Jorbon about his reasons for resigning. Smolka also spoke with Senator Litokwa Tomeing from Wotje, Carmen Bigler, Shiro Riklon, Carl Ingram, and with other members of the voter-education task forces, including commission member Amatlein Kabua Heine and task force members Nejan Edwards, Nag Nang, Ina Lomae, Andrew Bilimon, and Gloriana Harris.

The third and most extensive visit was made on September 1–11, 1983, to observe the conduct of the plebiscite. Howard Penniman and Richard Smolka went to Majuro, David Butler went first to Kwajalein and then to Majuro, and Austin Ranney and Raymond Wolfinger went first to the East-West Center at the University of Hawaii and then to Kwajalein and Ebeye. Wolfinger also went to Wotho and Rongelap on election day.

The Majuro team had further discussions with many of the election officials and political leaders met on earlier trips, especially Carmen Bigler, Shiro Riklon, Carl Ingram, George Allen, and Senator Henchi Balos of Bikini. The team also visited the headquarters of the anticompact coalition and attended a class on the compact taught by Brother Henry Schwalbenberg.

The Kwajalein team spent much of its time on Ebeye discussing the election arrangements with Hermios Kibin and voter-education issues with Kwajalein atoll's main anticompact leaders, including Senators Imada Kabua and Ataji Balos, Mayor Alvin Jacklick, and Fountain Inok, president of the Ebeye Chamber of Commerce. They also had discussions with the two main procompact leaders on Ebeye, Damien Ishoda and Sato Maie. On Kwajalein discussions were held with Andrik Niteak, *iroij* (traditional chief) of Enniburr Island; Jiba Kabua, Repmar's main liaison officer for Kwajalein; Lynn K. Lanej, chief precinct official for Kwajalein Island; and Paul Patrick, head of the union of Marshallese workers for KMR. On election day, Butler, Ranney, and Wolfinger observed the voting on Ebeye and Kwajalein. Wolfinger also observed the voting on Wotho and Rongelap. Penniman, Smolka, and Butler observed voting on Majuro and were also present during the first two days of the vote counting in Majuro, where the votes from all the voting districts were counted and tallied. On their trips to and from the Marshall Islands, Penniman, Smolka, Ranney, and Wolfinger visited the East-West Center at the University of Hawaii and participated in discussions on Marshallese culture and politics with Micronesia experts Norman Meller and Leonard Mason.

Much of the analysis that follows is based upon these discussions as well as upon documentary materials collected by the scholars.

Preliminaries to the Plebiscite

Negotiation of the Compact. The negotiations between the Marshall Islands and the United States over the content of the compact and the related agreements encountered many difficulties, especially in connection with the vexing issues of compensating the Kwajalein landowners and settling the claims of Marshallese injured by the nuclear testing. As a result, the negotiations were even more protracted and difficult than those with Palau and far more difficult than those with the FSM. The breakthrough in the Marshallese-U.S. negotiations finally came in late June 1983, when both sides agreed upon a new formula for U.S. payments to the Repmar government for settling the nuclear-damage claims. Originally the United States had proposed that it would pay approximately $150 million over a fifteen-year period. Repmar said that the amount was too small, but the United

81

States refused to increase it. Then it was proposed that the United States pay the entire $150 million at the *beginning* of free association, so that the money could be invested and produce returns expected to be about $18 million a year. At the end of the fifteen years the principal and interest from investment would add up to an estimated total payment of $270 million, considerably more than the original proposal, without requiring any additional appropriations by the United States. Both sides agreed to settle the claims in this way, and on June 25, 1983, President Amata Kabua signed the compact for Repmar and Ambassador Fred Zeder signed it for the United States. Soon thereafter the plebiscite date was set for September 7 by the *Nitijela,* the Marshallese parliament.

The Timing of the Plebiscite. As in Palau and the FSM, some opponents of the compact argued that the September 7 date was too early. The compact, they said, is nearly 300 pages long and packed with obscure legal language; the voters need much more than the two-and-a-half months allotted to study and understand it. The procompact leaders replied that the main issues in the compact had been discussed for at least thirteen years and were well understood by most Marshallese. Furthermore, the political education program and the campaigning by the organizations supporting and opposing the compact, with the generous news coverage in the *Marshall Islands Journal* and the government radio station, would provide extensive additional details. Hence postponing the election was unnecessary.

AEI's scholars agreed with the conclusion of the United Nations observers that

> although some people informed us that they did not understand the compact, we believe that, very largely as a result of the programme of political education, in general the people of the Marshall Islands were able to cast their votes on 7 September 1983 with a knowledge of the major issues involved and with at least some idea of the possible alternative constitutional options. [1]

There is no reason to suppose that postponing the vote another two or three months would have significantly increased popular understanding.

The Wording of the Ballot. In preparing the wording of the ballot, the U.S. and Repmar negotiators had the Palauan and FSM ballots and experiences as models, both good and bad. There was little controversy over the propositions' wording. The ballot was printed in both English and Marshallese, and it read as in figure 4–1.

FIGURE 4–1

OFFICIAL BALLOT, PLEBISCITE ON FUTURE POLITICAL STATUS
MARSHALL ISLANDS, 1983

PART ONE

TO VOTE ON THE QUESTION OF FREE ASSOCIATION WITH THE UNITED STATES, PUT AN "X" OR OTHER MARK IN ONE OF THE TWO BOXES.

DO YOU APPROVE OF THE COMPACT OF FREE ASSOCIATION AND ITS RELATED AGREEMENTS?

☐ YES/AET

☐ NO/JAB

PART TWO

THE VOTER IS ALSO REQUESTED TO VOTE ON THE QUESTION IN THIS PART. TO VOTE ON THE QUESTION IN THIS PART, PUT AN "X" OR OTHER MARK IN ONE OF THE TWO BOXES.

☐ INDEPENDENCE

☐ A RELATIONSHIP WITH THE UNITED STATES OTHER THAN FREE ASSOCIATION

YOU MAY DESCRIBE THAT STATUS:

....
....
....

Any ballot marked by a voter for either of these propositions was regarded as valid and was counted. As in Palau and the FSM, the answers to the first question were binding, and the answers to the second question were advisory. The Marshallese ballot followed its two predecessors by specifying "independence" as one of the options in part 2. The other alternatives were not specified because it was felt that such a list might arbitrarily structure the voters' preferences, and the advisory nature of part 2 made listing specific options less important. The options that in fact received the most discussion and were most often marked on the ballot were "commonwealth," "sticker," "statehood," and "status quo." The "sticker" option was unique to the Marshall Islands plebiscite and merits some further explanation.

The "Sticker" Option. One of the strongest elements in the coalition opposing the compact consisted of those Marshallese and their attorneys who were making claims, or intended to make claims, against the United States for personal injuries and property damages incurred as a result of the testing of nuclear weapons by the United States in the late 1940s and early 1950s.

Section 177 of the compact and its related agreement proposed to handle these suits and any future suits by having the United States pay to Repmar a sum of money that would cumulate to $270 million over fifteen years. Repmar would decide how much in damages would be paid to particular individuals, the suits before the courts would be dropped, and no future suits would be brought. The nuclear-victims element within the anticompact coalition, as organized by MIATLP, was strongly opposed to this provision and felt its defeat was important enough to warrant defeating the whole compact.

A typical anticompact newspaper advertisement published before the election said:

> We believe that for whatever reason you might vote yes you still might not believe that a 177 Agreement which provides so little money for all of the radiation victims AND for the clean up on Bikini is fair. . . . There is a place on the ballot for you to write in or put in what you think. No matter whether you vote yes or vote no you should use this opportunity to tell the United States Congress how you personally feel. We have provided stickers to place on the ballot, a copy of which appears with this article. Please peel off the back and stick it on the bottom of the ballot: NO to 177 or JAB 177. . . . No matter how you vote, yes or no [on part 1], please use this method to Vote Jab on 177.[2]

The exact language of the sticker was

> A Compact of Free Association should NOT include a 177 Agreement. Radiation victims should be FREE to settle PRIVATELY or go to Court.

How this novel method of voting worked out on election day will be described later.

The Voter-Education Program

The voter-education program in the Marshall Islands was funded by the United States and administered by a five-member Commission of Public Education on the Draft Compact of Free Association. The commission's members were appointed by the Repmar cabinet in November 1982. The chairperson was Carmen Bigler, secretary of the Department of Internal Affairs (an appointed, not elected, position), and the other commissioners were divided equally between proponents and opponents of the compact: Amatlein Kabua Heine and

Abner Lomae represented the Aet (Yes) forces, and Jack Jorbon and Laninruj Abon represented the Jab (No) forces.

The commission began the program by having the compact translated into Marshallese and printed in both English (5,000 copies) and Marshallese (15,000 copies). Even with only one indigenous language involved (as opposed to three in Palau and eight in the FSM), the task was not without its technical difficulties: a Marshallese involved in the translation told us that at one point the provision in English that the United States would give "sympathetic consideration" to future Repmar requests for funding was translated into Marshallese as giving "sorrowful amazement" to the requests. Arguably, the spirit of the translation was more accurate than the letter, but it was changed. When the translation was complete, the commission appointed twenty-four persons to the Voter Education Task Force, brought them to Majuro for a two-week training session on the meaning of each section of the compact, and prepared them to go to all of Repmar's populated places to distribute copies of the compact and to answer questions about its contents.

In February 1983 the commission ran out of funds, and the negotiations over the nuclear claims provisions of the compact became deadlocked. It was not clear when the plebiscite would be held. Consequently the voter-education program was suspended for several months. It was reactivated in late June immediately after the terms of the compact were finally agreed upon and the date for the plebiscite was set.

In mid-July the two opposition members of the commission, Jack Jorbon and Laninruj Abon, resigned. They charged that they had not been consulted on the appointment of the members of the task force, that an American clergyman (Brother Henry Schwalbenberg, S.J.) should not be participating in the voter-education program, and that Chairperson Bigler had taken many actions without their knowledge or consent.[3]

Richard Smolka made a special trip to Majuro on August 8–14 to inquire into the matter. He discussed the situation at length with Jack Jorbon and Carmen Bigler. Jorbon said that his major complaint was that the voter-education program did not even try to explain the advantages and disadvantages of the various alternatives to the compact but talked only about the contents of the compact. He felt that the commonwealth alternative, among others, should be fully explained to and discussed with the voters. He did not question the accuracy of any of the commission's or the task force's written or oral explanations of any provision of the compact.

Carmen Bigler replied that not only had all the members of the commission been informed of all of the commission's decisions but had participated in making them, and she specifically included in this information the naming of the task force members and the invitation to Brother Henry to participate in the program. She added that from the beginning everyone had understood that the program's proper function was to make certain that the voters understood the provisions of the compact, since that is what they would be voting on. That job by itself was very demanding, she said, and the commission had neither the time nor the resources to give full attention to the compact and to each of its possible alternatives.

After these interviews and a review of what the task force was doing, Smolka concluded that the voter-education program was not being used to propagandize for Yes votes, that the opposition had a full and fair opportunity to put its views before the voters, and that the opposition was making full use of its opportunities in radio broadcasts, newspaper advertisements, and rallies in the main population centers.

The commission reported just before the election that it had conducted 129 community meetings with a total known attendance of 4,495, which represented about 35 percent of the estimated number of voters eligible to vote in the plebiscite. Teams visited nearly every populated place in the Marshall Islands and also met with Marshallese students in Hawaii and in four cities on the mainland.[4]

The commission's efforts were supplemented by a series of radio talks made by Oscar de Brum, the chief secretary, and by Brother Henry Schwalbenberg both of whom explained the compact section by section. As discussed in chapter 3 Brother Henry, an American Jesuit with graduate training in economics and political science from Columbia University, had conducted analyses, courses, and seminars on the compact in the FSM. In the Marshall Islands he assisted the commission in preparing its explanation of the compact, taught an evening course open to anyone who wished to attend, and thus played a major role in the voter-education program. As he had in the FSM, he regarded his proper role as one of objectively setting forth the meaning and consequences of the compact by comparing it with the other alternatives. Contrary to the criticisms of Jack Jorbon, Brother Henry's presentations dealt at some length with the nature, advantages, and disadvantages of both independence and commonwealth status (as exemplified by the experience of the Northern Marianas), on the ground that they were the most likely alternatives to free association. Some anticompact forces declared that it was not proper for an American—and a clergyman at that—to take part in the voter-education program. AEI's scholars, however, like most outside observers, felt that Brother Henry's presentations were accurate and fair accounts of the facts and probabilities, that they were not briefs for either side, and that they played a valuable role in the voter-education program.

Public meetings on the compact were held in every Marshallese community within the Marshalls, and in the principal Marshallese communities outside the islands in Guam, Palau, the FSM, Hawaii, and the mainland United States. Twice each day from August 15 to September 3 the government radio in Majuro broadcast discussions of the compact, with equal time made available to the procompact and anticompact forces, and the number of programs was stepped up in the week before the election. For observers on the spot it was difficult to travel far without observing people listening to the radio discussions of the compact, so apparently the discussions were widely heard by an attentive audience.

In addition, for at least forty days before the vote the *Marshall Islands Journal*, which has a circulation of about 1,700, announced on its masthead the number of days remaining until the plebiscite: "Journal Countdown: Forty Days until the Plebiscite." The newspaper devoted extensive coverage to the campaign, printed short explanations of the various provisions, and published many statements by the leaders of both sides. It also carried numerous full-page advertisements against the compact purchased by the "Vote Jab" forces. AEI's scholars concluded that the voter-education program made a major effort to acquaint the Marshallese people with the compact's provisions, that the Marshallese had an unusually good opportunity to become informed about the issues, and that many of them did so. Indeed, rarely do public issues in the initiative and referendum elections held by many of the states of the United States command such thorough coverage and attention.

The Campaign

The Anticompact Coalition. In the Marshall Islands the opposition to the compact was, as in Palau but not in the FSM, well organized, highly visible, and very active. It was conducted by a coalition of three elements, each with a somewhat different motive for trying to defeat the compact.

The first element was MIATLP, which was concerned almost exclusively with blocking the compact's provisions in section 177 to settle all nuclear claims with money to be distributed by the fund manager and to require that all suits by individuals against the United States in U.S. courts be dropped. Richard Gerry, an American lawyer representing MIATLP, took the lead in preparing and financing many full-page advertisements in the *Marshall Islands Journal* attacking the compact. He also appeared on radio, on television, and at public meetings to attack section 177. Part of his time was spent in explaining, rather defensively, that the 25 percent contingency-fee basis on which he and his associates were representing their Marshallese clients was a common and entirely respectable financial arrangement in U.S. legal practice. Indeed, he said, 33 percent is the usual basis but had been lowered in these cases because they were suing the U.S. government. His emphasis on this subject and his frequent appearances may have made his role more prominent in the Jab campaign than its Marshallese leaders would have preferred: one of the most-displayed procompact banners read: "DROWN ALL LAWYERS (MIATLP) AND VOTE *FOR* THE COMPACT!"

The second element of the anticompact coalition was the Kwajalein Atoll Corporation (KAC), a group of Kwajalein landowners, led by Senators Imada Kabua and Ataji Balos from Kwajalein atoll, Kwajalein Mayor Alvin Jacklick, and Fountain Inok, president of the Kwajalein Chamber of Commerce. For several years before the plebiscite these leaders and the landowners they represented had grown increasingly dissatisfied with the rents that the United States was paying for the use of their land for the missile range facilities and increasingly resentful of the KMR's security arrangements, which, in their view, made it unnecessarily difficult for the landowners to visit their own lands. They also protested the crowded and unsanitary living conditions on the island of Ebeye, where the Marshallese workers employed by KMR on Kwajalein had to live. From June to October 1982 these leaders had organized a "sail-in" protest, in which some Marshallese established camps at Kwajalein and Roi-Namur islands and also stationed boats in Kwajalein lagoon to prevent the United States from launching the missiles it was testing. President Amata Kabua and the other leaders of the Repmar government had opposed the protest, and the protesters finally withdrew. No serious incidents of violence erupted, but even so the episode left a residue of bitter feelings not only between the protesters and the United States but also between the protesters and the leaders of the Majuro government. A small group of Kwajalein landowners opposed the KAC and supported the Majuro government and the compact. They formed a counter-organization called the Kwajalein Independent Landowners, nicknamed "Ten-Ten" after the quick-service store for KMR workers on Kwajalein Island—suggesting that they were lackeys of the Americans running KMR. They could muster, however, only a handful of votes, and KAC spoke for a large majority of Kwajalein atoll's voters.

The third element of the opposition coalition was a quasi-political party called the "Voice of the Marshalls." It consisted of a group of leaders, mainly from the southern atolls of Ebon, Jaluit, Mili, and Lib, who had unsuccessfully opposed the adoption of the new Marshallese constitution in 1979. Their leaders included Senators Litokwa Tomeing from Wotje, Chuji Chutaro from Mili, Carl Heine from Jaluit, Ekpap Silk from Ebon, and Evelyn Kanou from Jaluit. Since the early 1970s this group has been the main opposition to the Kabua regime in Majuro, and they have a long history of seeking strong political and economic ties with the United States. In the plebiscite campaign they took the position that the compact provided for too *great* a degree of separation of the Marshall Islands from the United States and put too much power in Repmar's hands. As longstanding opponents of President Amata Kabua and his *Allin Kein Ad* party, they believed that Repmar's new and increased powers under the compact would not be used fairly for the benefit of all the Marshallese islands and people, and they preferred commonwealth status. As Brother Henry Schwalbenberg sums up their position:

> Many opposition party members [believed] that strong political links with the United States would act as a brake on the power of President Kabua and the *iroij*. A commonwealth status under U.S. laws would not recognize the [traditional] Marshallese class distinctions, thus giving more clout to educated commoners. Furthermore, it would bring in more money, and this administered not by the elected government of the Marshall Islands but rather by Washington.[5]

This three-element coalition mounted a substantial campaign against the compact. Supported mainly by the financial backing of MIATLP and KAC, they published many full-page advertisements in the *Marshall Islands Journal*, spoke frequently on the government radio station, posted anticompact posters in all areas of opposition strength, distributed softball bats, T-shirts, and other campaign paraphernalia, and organized parades and rallies, the largest being held on Ebeye just before the election.

The opposition campaign themes were somewhat diluted in the final days, however, when an effort was made to persuade *all* voters, regardless of whether they intended to vote for or against the compact on part 1, to place the sticker on part 2 of the ballot. So doing, the opposition felt, would send the strongest possible signal to the U.S. and Repmar governments that the provisions of section 177 were not acceptable and that the rights of Marshallese citizens to sue the government of the United States in U.S. courts should not be given up.

The Campaign for the Compact. In one major respect the campaign in the Marshall Islands differed sharply from the campaigns in Palau and the FSM. As noted in earlier chapters, no substantial explicit procompact campaigns were mounted in either Palau or the FSM. That was not the case in the Marshall Islands. The procompact forces, led by President Amata Kabua and his *Allin Kein Ad* party, decided that the opposition forces were very strong and that the compact might lose unless a vigorous campaign were mounted on its behalf. So Oscar de Brum, the head of Repmar's civil service, led a government team to the southern atolls to win support for the compact. Charles Domnick, a cabinet minister from Maloelap, led a team to the northern atolls. Most important of all, President Amata Kabua made a month-long trip to eighteen atolls, including Enewetak, Kwajalein, Jabat, and Ailinglaplap, using his prowess on the electric organ and his oratorical skills to attract audiences and persuade them to vote for the compact. The procompact campaign climaxed in Majuro on the day before the election. A parade, consisting of private vehicles and Repmar trucks decorated with VOTE AET signs took more than a half-hour to pass. The parade was followed by an outdoor barbecue, drawing hundreds of people, some of whom remained until long after sunset. Posters supporting the compact emphasized the financial benefits it would bring and also hailed the chance to end centuries of rule by foreigners. One sign read: "We are not American Indians, we are Marshallese. This is the 20th century and we know better. VOTE AET!"

For both the Aet and Jab sides, however, there was a private and personal campaign as well as a public campaign. Each devoted much time and effort trying to persuade the *iroij* of the rightness of their side so that the *iroij* would, in turn, convince their followers to vote the right way. Leaders on both sides told AEI's scholars that, aside from some people in Majuro, most Marshallese would not be much influenced by the general propaganda of either side coming over the radio or in the newspaper advertisements. Most ordinary voters, they said, would be mainly influenced by what their traditional chiefs advised; hence persuading those chiefs was the prime, though not the only, objective of the campaigns of both sides. We shall note some manifestations of *iroij* influence in our analysis of the plebiscite results.

The Main Issues in the Campaign. The issues that received the most attention and discussion during the campaign were the following:

1. *Are section 177 and its related agreement an acceptable way to settle the nuclear victims' claims?* To understand this issue, one must first be

90

Brother Henry Schwalbenberg, David Butler, Austin Ranney, and UN observer Paul Poudade (L to R) waiting for the polls to open on Ebeye. The chief election officer had overslept, and the polls opened an hour late.

Checking the voter lists on Ebeye. Many residents of Ebeye were registered on other islands, and all had to have their names checked against special lists before they could vote. This made for long lines by the end of the day.

Above left: Voting on Ebeye. Most voters cast their ballots in outdoor plywood voting booths and deposited them in double-lidded ballot boxes such as those shown in the photograph. Above right: Taking the Kwajalein votes to the airplane for counting in Majuro. Wherever they were cast, all ballots were taken to Majuro for counting. Those cast on Kwajalein island were trucked to the airport and flown to Majuro after the polls had closed.

The polling place on Kwajalein island. The U.S. authorities at the Kwajalein Missile Range set up a special American-style polling place for their Micronesian workers, resulting in an unusually high turnout.

clear about the main provisions of the controversial section 177 agreement as negotiated by Repmar and the United States.

a. The agreement will settle all claims by the Marshallese people against the United States for injuries and damages resulting from the U.S. nuclear testing program.

b. On the day the compact becomes effective, the United States will pay to Repmar the sum of $150,000,000. This sum will be invested in a perpetual fund that will yield approximately $18,000,000 per year for each of the fifteen years of the agreement.

c. From these earnings, during the first fifteen years of the compact the people of the affected atolls will receive a guaranteed total of $183,750,000 in quarterly payments allocated as follows:

To the people of Bikini: $75,000,000
To the people of Enewetak: $48,750,000
To the people of Rongelap: $37,500,000
To the people of Utirik: $22,500,000

d. Also during the first fifteen years of the compact, a total of $45,750,000 will be set aside for payment of uncompensated claims from those atolls or any other atoll or island group in the Marshalls. A claims tribunal established by Repmar but independent of its executive and legislative officers will adjudicate all such uncompensated claims.

e. Espousal: this agreement constitutes the full settlement of all claims, past, present, and future, of the citizens and government of all the Marshall Islands against the United States which are based on the nuclear testing program. Repmar will terminate any and all legal proceedings in the courts of the Marshall Islands against the United States involving claims arising out of the nuclear testing program. No United States court will have jurisdiction to entertain such claims, and any such claim now pending in the U.S. courts will be dismissed.

Those were the main provisions of section 177. The procompact forces argued that the settlement was fair, that it was the best deal the United States was likely to make, and that a good settlement firmly in hand was far better than holding out for a higher but illusory settlement sometime in the future. Moreover, some preliminary decisions on the MIATLP suits in the U.S. courts had already indicated that most of the suits pending in 1983 and likely to be filed in the future would not be successful. Accordingly, procompact forces argued, section 177 was a much better settlement than any other the Marshallese people were likely to get.

The anticompact forces made two main arguments. First, the prospects for winning the nuclear-claims suits in the U.S. courts were much better than the procompact forces alleged, and pursuing the individual-claims strategy was likely to bring much more money to the victims than they would get from the section 177 settlement. (After all, those against the compact noted, the total damages being asked in the suits then pending came to more than $4 *billion*.) Second, section 177 violates the rights of individual Marshallese by taking away their right to sue for damages in the courts and forcing them to accept amounts decided by their local government council and the Repmar claims tribunal. In short: the nuclear claims litigants (and their attorneys) would get more money, which would be more fairly distributed, under the status quo than under the provisions of section 177.

2. *Are the provisions for the Kwajalein Missile Range land acceptable?* The KMR is by far the largest U.S. military installation in the entire Trust Territory. It is important to the U.S. weapons testing program, and it is also a major source of revenue for the Marshallese. Under agreements made prior to the compact, the United States makes annual payments of $7 million, plus other benefits, for the use of the land, and most of the money is distributed to the landowners according to Marshallese customary rules. KMR also employs about 500 Marshallese workers at U.S. wage scales (which are substantially higher than the rates of pay elsewhere in the Marshalls), and the Majuro government collects a 3 percent income tax on the American incomes earned at KMR. Brother Henry Schwalbenberg estimates that "roughly 30 percent of the Marshallese gross domestic product is derived from Kwajalein Missile Range in the form of land payments, taxes, and employment."[6]

The compact and related agreements propose to increase the annual payments for KMR from $7 million to $9 million, but they also have two provisions that are unacceptable to the KAC. First, the terms for the use of the KMR will not be renegotiated for thirty years, whereas at present the KMR agreement is renegotiated every two or three years. Second, the compact will convert what is now a series of short-term agreements between the United States and the Kwajalein landowners into a long-term agreement between the United States and the Majuro government. This provision has caused some members of the KAC to fear that Repmar will siphon off some of the money to finance projects elsewhere in the Marshalls. As Brother Henry comments, "it seems that trust is not taken for granted too often in the Marshall Islands."[7]

The procompact forces argued that the proposed rental money

and duration of the KMR agreement were fair, adequate, and the best deal the United States was likely to make. Moreover, they said, the many benefits of the compact for all the Marshallese people should not be denied or postponed because a few Kwajalein landowners think they can get more money.

The anticompact forces argued that the United States had already invested billions of dollars in the KMR facilities and were in no position to abandon them rather than pay more rent. Hence the landowners are in a better bargaining position than the United States, and Repmar should take better advantage of that fact than the compact allows. Moreover, the Jab forces argued, the land rights of the people of Kwajalein are their most precious possessions and represent the values held most dear by all Marshallese. To abridge their rights because uninvolved people in Majuro and the other islands are willing to sell them out for the compact's alleged benefits is unjust and unacceptable.

3. *What future status is best for the Marshall Islands?* The procompact side argued that free association is clearly better than any of the realistic alternatives. It is better than continuing the trusteeship because it ends the demeaning semicolonial status the Marshallese people have known for too long. It is better than independence because the Marshall Islands are not capable of surviving economically by themselves, and they will need massive U.S. economic aid and military protection into the indefinite future. It is better than commonwealth because it gives the Marshallese control of almost all of their own affairs, far more than the people of the Northern Marianas have. Moreover, the compact removes any possibility (which would be ever-present in commonwealth status) that the United States might use its power of eminent domain to claim ownership of Marshallese lands. It is better than being a territory of the United States because it makes the Marshall Islands sovereign over their own affairs, especially in matters concerning land ownership. Finally, it is better than statehood for the same reasons, and, in any case, statehood is not likely to be granted by the U.S. Congress.

For reasons given above, the "Voice of the Marshalls" opposition in the southern atolls opposed the very principle of free association and preferred commonwealth or some other closer relation with the United States. Few people in the other two opposition groups opposed the *principle* of free association in favor of some other principle, such as independence, commonwealth, or statehood. Almost all of the opposition favored *free association on better terms*. As noted above, they favored especially the elimination or radical revision of section 177 and a drastic revision of the terms affecting the KMR lands.

Hence they favored rejecting this particular compact and then negotiating a new and better compact they could support.

In short, for most Marshallese the choice was between accepting this compact on these terms now or continuing the trusteeship for a while longer in the hope that a better deal could be struck with the United States and a better compact of free association could be approved in the future.

Election Experience and Rules

Previous Election Experience. Like Palau and the FSM, the Marshall Islands had already held several elections before 1983. There were major referendums in 1974, 1977, 1978, and 1979. Observers sent to the latter two by the United Nations Trusteeship Council praised the way the referendums were conducted. In addition, there were elections for members of the Congress of Micronesia every two years from 1964 through 1976, elections for members of constitutional conventions in 1974 and 1979, and elections for members of the *Nitijela* in 1979 (another *Nitijela* election was held in November 1983 after the plebiscite on the compact). Therefore the Marshallese people had had much experience with both candidate and referendum elections before September 1983, and Repmar had assembled a body of officials with considerable expertise in administering all aspects of elections, including registration, absentee voting, and the casting and counting of votes.

The Rules. The 1983 plebsicite was conducted under rules laid down by the *Nitijela* and administered by Repmar's chief electoral officer, Shiro E. Riklon.

A citizen of the Marshall Islands was qualified to vote if he or she was eighteen years of age or older on the day of the plebiscite, had fulfilled the requirements for registration, and was not under a judgment of mental incompetence or insanity, on parole or probation, or under sentence for a felony.

Most eligible Marshallese were already listed on the voter registration rolls from previous elections; but, to encourage maximum participation by unregistered yet otherwise eligible citizens, registration at the polls on election day was also permitted. In addition, all citizens had the option of being registered either where they resided or where they had land rights, though not, of course, at both places.

The *Nitijela* also passed a new and less demanding absentee voting law. It retained absentee voting by mail and added a new system of "on-island" absentee voting, which allowed citizens to vote in person rather than by mail, at districts in the Marshalls other than those in which they were registered. It also allowed "off-island" absentee voting, which authorized the chief electoral officer to appoint special election-board members empowered to notarize registration and absentee-voting affidavits in locations outside the Marshalls, such as Saipan, Guam, Ponape, Palau, Honolulu, and Huntington Beach, California.

The deadline for registration outside the Marshall Islands was August 24, 1983, and absentee ballots could be requested until August 28. Within the Marshall Islands, absentee ballots could be requested until September 2, five days before the election. The deadline for receipt of absentee ballots was election day, whether delivered by mail or by hand to a member of the board of elections or deposited in a ballot container.

The chief electoral officer was responsible for printing the ballots and for delivering an adequate number of them, in sealed packages, to the members of the election boards, whom he had appointed for each polling station.

On election day, eighty-five polling stations were open throughout the Marshall Islands. At each station, when persons wishing to vote appeared, their names were checked on the registration rolls and, if they were on the rolls and had not voted earlier, they were given ballots. In addition to the standard polling places equipped with plywood voting booths, three "mobile polls" were established for voting in the rural areas of Majuro. One team of election officials traveled in an automobile and two teams used trucks, with a policeman accompanying each vehicle. Using the list of registered voters, the poll officials moved from house to house processing voters and having them mark their ballots and deposit them in regular ballot boxes. The three mobile polls covered about thirty-two kilometers of Majuro's fifty-eight kilometer length. Poll watchers (thirty representing the government and eighty representing the anticompact coalition) as well as press and official observers were present at many of the polling stations and mobile polls.

Most of the election-day registrants voted on Majuro and Ebeye. These voters used a double-envelope procedure and cast their ballots in the same manner provided for those whose right to vote was challenged. In this procedure, the voter marked and placed his ballot in an envelope that was put inside a second envelope, which contained the voter's name, address, and voting district. If there was no challenge to the voter's right to vote and no evidence that he had voted at another location, then the envelope with the ballot was separated from the affidavit and placed with others to be counted later.

The polls were scheduled to open at 7:00 a.m. and did so in Majuro and most other locations. When the AEI and UN observers arrived at the polling place on Ebeye at 6:45 a.m., however, they found neither set-up voting booths nor election officials. The observers were told that the person in charge had overslept and would be there shortly. Eventually the officials arrived, the plywood voting booths were hastily assembled, and at 8:00 a.m. the voting began.

In both Ebeye and Majuro the election authorities underestimated the number of election-day registrations and of in-person absentee voters, and, as a result, the voting lines began to build early and grew longer and longer as the day wore on. The polls were scheduled to close at 7:00 p.m., but when that time arrived several hundred people were still standing in line at the places designated for absentee voting and for election-day registration. Consequently the chief electoral officer decided to keep the polls open at both places until every voter standing in line at 7:00 p.m. had a chance to vote. (Policemen were stationed at the end of the lines to make sure that no one joined them after 7:00 p.m.) The polls finally closed around midnight in Majuro and around 1:30 a.m. in Ebeye.

All the ballot boxes from the eighty-five polling stations throughout the islands were brought, some by airplane and some by boat, to the *Nitijela* building in Majuro for counting; there was no counting of any kind elsewhere. Because of the distances involved, all the boxes were not assembled in Majuro until September 10, three days after the voting. Nevertheless the count began with a prayer shortly after 10:00 a.m. on September 8. Two ballot-counting teams processed and tallied the ballots in full view of all observers, including representatives of both the procompact and anticompact sides, United Nations observers, AEI scholars, and journalists. The count began with the Majuro boxes. The counting teams first unfolded and counted the number of ballots, checking the totals against the number reported. Absentee voters as well as election-day registrants were checked against the voter registration rolls to ensure that none voted twice. The teams then began a standard "call-and-tally" procedure, whereby two counters scrutinized each ballot and then called the votes on the questions to the tabulators and the tabulators made the appropriate marks on the tally sheets. The boxes from Majuro and Ebeye, which had by far the most absentee and election-day registrants, took the longest to process.

The stickers pasted on part 2 of certain ballots initially posed some problems for the counters, who had not seen anything like them in previous elections. Not unreasonably, it was decided to count and tally them simply as "stickers" rather than to classify them

96

as an alternative form of association with the United States comparable to the independence or commonwealth alternatives. All blank
ballots on part 2 were also duly recorded and tallied.

The procedure was careful, demanding, and slow. The count
continued all day Thursday, Friday, and Saturday and was not completed until more than a week after the voting.

AEI's scholars concluded that, although the administration of the
plebiscite sometimes fell short of perfect efficiency (witness, for example, the long lines and late poll closings in Majuro and Ebeye) there
was no evidence of fraud and the election was as "clean" as most
elections in the United States and other Western democracies.
Moreover, both the election rules and their administration were designed to make it convenient for all eligible persons to vote. Like the
UN observers, AEI's scholars were greatly impressed by the good
humor, orderliness, and devotion to democratic values shown by the
many voters in Majuro and Ebeye who stood in lines—many for
hours in hot sun and high humidity or in evening and nightime
darkness—to cast their votes. AEI scholars have no doubt that the
plebiscite's results represented a fair reflection of the preferences of
the Marshallese people.

The Plebiscite Results

The plebiscite results, listed by voting districts, are shown in table
4–1.

Turnout. At the time of the plebiscite there were approximately
13,000 registered voters in the Marshall Islands. A total of 10,724
persons cast valid ballots, and an additional 127 persons went to the
polls but had their ballots rejected for improper marking. Thus the
turnout in the 1983 plebiscite was 83.5 percent. By mainland U.S.
standards the turnout was remarkably high, and it was considerably
higher than both the 49.3 percent turnout in the 1979 referendum on
the proposed constitution for the Marshall Islands and the 59.5 percent turnout in the 1978 referendum on the proposed Micronesia-
wide constitution.

Analysis of the Results: Part 1. Perhaps the first characteristic of the
vote on part 1 of the ballot ("Do you approve of the Compact of Free
Association and its related agreements?") was the heavy majorities
for one side or the other in almost every district, as is shown by the
data in table 4–2. The figures show that in only six of the twenty-four
voting districts did the size of the majority for one side or the other

97

TABLE 4-1

RESULTS OF THE MARSHALL ISLANDS PLEBISCITE BY DISTRICT, 1983

Electoral District	Part 1			Part 2					
	Yes	No	% Yes	Independence	Commonwealth	Sticker	Not specified	Other	Blank
Ailinglaplap	434	208	67.6	29	9	16	38	1	550
Ailuk	237	93	71.8	16	1	56	28	0	230
Arno	581	175	76.9	46	1	26	71	1	611
Aur	219	72	75.3	16	4	25	18	1	227
Ebon	104	370	21.9	15	175	63	32	0	191
Enewetak-Ujelang	185	63	74.6	7	0	5	6	0	230
Jabat	46	11	80.7	2	1	4	3	0	47
Jaluit	268	595	31.0	28	167	115	141	4	411
Kili-Bikini	65	241	21.2	4	0	5	5	0	292
Kwajalein	418	993	29.6	44	1	341	150	1	876
Lae	103	36	74.1	4	0	12	6	0	117

Lib	30	39	43.5	3	0	5	6	0	56
Likiep	274	95	74.3	16	1	46	27	0	281
Majuro	1,491	417	78.1	135	14	148	175	1	1,440
Maloelap	255	184	58.1	18	2	116	19	1	283
Mejit	210	47	81.7	11	4	32	28	1	182
Mili	182	306	37.3	19	13	35	46	0	375
Namorik	233	99	70.2	6	1	17	20	0	288
Namu	322	15	95.5	11	0	5	7	1	313
Rongelap	16	95	14.4	2	0	84	0	0	25
Ujae	110	25	81.5	8	0	7	8	0	112
Utirik	145	56	72.1	2	0	38	5	0	157
Wotho	44	16	73.2	2	0	5	4	0	49
Wotje	127	206	38.1	9	4	110	22	0	189
Postal									
absentees	116	52	69.0	21	6	1	68	2	70
Total	6,215	4,509	58.0	474	404	1,317	933	14	7,602

SOURCE: Official report of the vote as certified by Shiro E. Riklon, chief electoral officer of the Marshall Islands, in a letter to Ambassador John Margetson, president, United Nations Trusteeship Council, January 24, 1984. See also Henry M. Schwalbenberg, S.J., "The Marshallese Plebiscite: No to Commonwealth" (Micronesia Seminar Memorandum 13, April 1984), table 1, p. 2, which differs slightly in the count of votes on part 2.

TABLE 4–2

SIZE OF PLEBISCITE MAJORITIES
IN MARSHALL ISLANDS VOTING DISTRICTS, 1983

	Districts with Yes Majorities	Districts with No Majorities
Total	16	8
Size of Majority		
50–59%	1	1
60–69%	1	3
70–79%	10	3
80–89%	3	1
90% and over	1	0
Mean Majority	75.4%	70.3%

SOURCE: Figures in table 4–1.

fall below 70 percent, and the average district majority for the sixteen districts voting Yes was 75.4 percent, while the average majority for the eight districts voting No was 70.3 percent. Hence the overall Yes majority of 57.9 percent was not the result of similar and evenly divided preferences throughout the islands; rather it resulted from the greater number of strongly Yes districts than of strongly No districts.

Most observers felt that these lopsided majorities for both sides reflected a basic feature of voting in Micronesia noted several times in preceding chapters: when the traditional chief or chiefs (in the case of the Marshall Islands, the *iroij* and *iroij laplaps*) have indicated their preferences on an issue, most of their followers vote accordingly—not because they fear reprisal but simply because they trust their chiefs to guide them in such matters.

When the returns are analyzed district by district, the components of support and rejection for the compact stand out.[8] We noted earlier that the anticompact coalition had three main elements. One element was the Kwajalein landowners and their attorneys; and Kwajalein, with a heavy turnout, voted 70.4 percent No and provided over one-fifth of all the No votes.

The second element was the "nuclear victims" group in the northern atolls spearheaded by MIATLP. The four "radiation atolls" mentioned by name in the compact were all generally expected to vote heavily against it; but, to the surprise of many observers, they split: Kili-Bikini voted 78.8 percent No and Rongelap voted 85.6 percent No (the largest No majority in any district). But Enewetak-

Ulejang voted 74.6 percent Yes, and Utirik voted 72.1 percent Yes. Together the four atolls produced a No majority of only 52.5 percent—an outcome that was both unexpected and extremely disappointing for the MIATLP forces. The other northern atolls with potential nuclear-damage claimants were also expected to produce large No votes, but they too dashed MIATLP's hopes: five of the six (Ailuk, Lae, Likiep, Mejit, and Wotho) produced strong Yes majorities, and only Wotje voted No.

The third element of the anticompact coalition was the "Voice of the Marshalls" group centered mainly in the southern atolls of Jaluit, Mili, Ebon, and Lib. All four voted strongly against the compact, with No majorities ranging from 78.1 percent in Ebon to 56.5 percent in Lib. Together they provided the largest single block of No votes—29 percent of the overall total compared to Kwajalein's 22 percent. These four atolls also produced the only substantial support for the "closer ties to the United States" option in part 2 of the ballot: together they contributed 355 of the overall total of 404 votes for closer ties and a majority of 55.6 percent compared with 30.7 percent among all voters.

Elsewhere the outcomes represented a major achievement for the procompact forces—especially impressive since a month before the plebiscite many knowledgeable observers expected the compact to lose. On heavily populated Majuro the forces led by President Kabua increased their majority from the 64.6 percent they had won in the 1979 referendum on the new constitution to 78.1 percent on the compact. Even in the southern atolls they increased: in 1979 they won an aggregate share of only 23.9 percent, but in 1983 it rose to 30.8 percent. In the other districts the Kabua forces either held or increased their 1979 majorities. Most observers credited the turnaround in the vote to the vigorous and skillful campaign waged by Secretary Oscar de Brum, Minister Charles Domnick, and, above all, President Amata Kabua in the crucial weeks just before the plebiscite.

Analysis of the Results: Part 2. As the figures in table 4–1 show, fully 70.7 percent of the voters did not vote on part 2 at all. For them the issue clearly was the acceptance or rejection of the compact; and, having expressed themselves on that question in part 1, they did not care to vote on part 2, which was, after all, only advisory.

Nevertheless, 29.3 percent of the voters did vote on part 2, and the distribution of their preferences tells us something about the state of opinion among the voters. The options of independence and commonwealth status each received support from less than 5 percent of the voters. Another 8.7 percent checked the box for "a relationship with the United States other than free association" but did not write any description on the lines provided for that purpose. The opposition coalition did persuade 1,317 voters (12.3 percent of the total) to mark the "other relationship" option and then paste the sticker against section 177 on the ballot.

Only four groups of voters—those in Ebon, Jaluit, Rongelap, and the postal absentee voters—cast more than 50 percent of their votes for the "other relationship" option of part 2. Of these, 61 percent of voters in Ebon cast their part 2 votes for commonwealth status, and only 22 percent used the sticker. In Jaluit 37 percent of voters cast their part 2 votes for commonwealth status, 31 percent did not specify an alternative, and 25 percent used the sticker. Only Rongelap voted solidly as MIATLP had urged: of the island's 111 total votes, 86 voters marked "other relationship;" and, of those, 84 voters—76 percent of all voters and 98 percent of all part 2 voters—pasted the sticker on their ballots. The postal absentees provided the only noteworthy votes for the "independence" option. Of the 168 voters in this group, 98 (58 percent) marked "other relationship" on part 2, and of those 21 marked "independence" as their preferred alternative—12.5 percent of all voters and 21 percent of those who marked part 2.

Although the sticker option also fared relatively well in Wotje, Kwajalein, Maloelap, and Utirik, the main message from the voting on part 2 was that the great majority of the Marshallese voters saw the plebiscite mainly as an opportunity to express their views on the compact.

The Effect of Absentee Voting and Election-Day Registration. We noted earlier that to make voting on the compact as convenient as possible, the *Nitijela* allowed a voter registered in one district to vote absentee in-person in another district on election day and also allowed an unregistered but otherwise eligible citizen to register at a polling place on election day. These liberalizing provisions had some noteworthy effects on both the turnout and the outcome, as shown in table 4–3. The figures there show that only slightly more than half of all votes were cast by persons voting in person in their home districts. Nearly a third of the voters voted in person in districts other than their home districts, and 14 percent of the votes were cast by persons who registered at the polls on election day.

The figures in table 4–3 also show that the election-day registrants were somewhat less in favor of the compact (53.4 percent Yes) than previously registered voters (58.7 percent Yes). It seems, first, that both liberalizing measures significantly increased the turnout and, second, that election-day registration helped the No forces while easier absentee voting helped the Yes forces. All four classes of voters

102

TABLE 4–3

Voting on Part 1 by Absentee Voters and Election-Day Registrants in the Marshall Islands Plebiscite, 1983

Type of Voting	Yes	No	Total	% Yes	% Total Votes
In person in home district	3,358	2,397	5,855	58.3	53.7
In-person absentee in another election district	1,942	1,362	3,304	58.8	30.8
Absentee by mail	116	52	168	69.0	1.6
Election-day registrant	799	698	1,497	53.4	13.9
Total	6,215	4,509	10,824	58.0	100.0

Source: Same as for table 4–1.

returned majorities in favor of the compact, however, so the liberalizing measures certainly did not determine the outcome.

Fairness of the Plebiscite

In the opinion of AEI's scholars, the Marshall Islands plebiscite was a fair election, and the result was a meaningful expression of the will of the Marshallese voters. The compact and the issues it posed were aired intensively on the radio for more than two months preceding the election, and most of the issues had been discussed for years before that. Both the procompact and anticompact forces had full access to newspapers, radio, and television, and both were able to use free time as well as purchased space to communicate their views. Both sides conducted peaceful major election-eve rallies.

The election rules and their application by the election officials were structured so that every Marshallese citizen, whether in his or her own district, in another district, or overseas, was able to register and vote with minimum difficulty. Although the administration of the casting and counting of votes on election day could have been conducted more efficiently with more election officials, no one who wanted to vote was denied the opportunity to do so. The patience of voters in Majuro and Ebeye, some of whom waited without complaint until past midnight to vote, was truly impressive.

The vote count was slow but deliberate and careful. Although the tally proceeded more slowly than necessary, the outcome of the vote, especially on part 1, was an accurate expression of opinions on that key question. There was some laxity in tallying preferences on part 2. This looseness was due, in some degree, to the great emphasis placed on part 1 (which, after all, was the action part of the plebiscite), and, in some degree, to the complications in interpreting, classifying, and tallying the variety of answers on part 2. Even so, when confronted with the novel use of stickers on the ballots, the chief electoral officer, in consultation with the attorney general, came to the sensible conclusion that the stickers should be accepted and tallied as expressions of a significant preference, even though their common message was apparently irrelevant to the question asked in part 2.

One of AEI's scholars summed up the plebiscite thus:

> It was a fair election. The U.N., in deciding whether their last trusteeship . . . can be abandoned, will certainly be told by its observers that the vote was an honest expression of an unglamorous, pragmatic choice.[9]

Notes

1. *Report of the United Nations Visiting Mission to Observe the Plebiscite in the Marshall Islands, Trust Territory of the Pacific Islands, September 1983* (United Nations Document T/1865, 1984), p. 5.

2. *Marshall Islands Journal* (September 2, 1983), p. 7.

3. *Marshall Islands Journal* (July 22, 1983), p. 1.

4. *Marshall Islands Journal* (August 30, 1983), p. 1, and (September 9, 1983), p. 1.

5. Henry M. Schwalbenberg, S.J., "The Marshallese Plebiscite: No to Commonwealth," Micronesia Seminar Memorandum #13 (April 1984), p. 5.

6. *Ibid.*, p. 6.

7. *Ibid.*, pp. 6–7.

8. For a more detailed district-by-district analysis, see *ibid.*, *passim.*

9. David Butler, *The Times* (London) (September 14, 1983), p. 14.

5

Referendums in Traditional Societies

We have approached our study of the Micronesian plebiscites of 1983 with at least two clear biases. First, we believe that democracy is the best form of government people have ever known—not perfect, not ideal, not flawless; just better than any known alternative. Second, we believe that free elections are the key institutions of democratic government, whether they are candidate elections, plebiscites, or other kinds of referendums. As we have written elsewhere: "The electoral process lies at the heart of democratic government, and the critical difference between democratic and nondemocratic regimes is to be found in whether or not they hold elections and, if they do, what kind."[1] Given these inclinations, the core question of our study of the Micronesian plebiscites remains: To what extent did those plebiscites measure up to the standards of a model democratic referendum? Before we give our answers we briefly set forth our conception of what those standards are.

Standards for Democratic Referendums

A plebiscite is a particular kind of referendum, and a referendum is one of the two basic types of democratic elections (the other being a candidate election, in which voters choose among candidates for public office). We believe that most of those who are concerned with this study's essential concerns will agree that a democratic referendum is one that lives up to at least the following standards:[2]

- The proposition or propositions on the ballot are phrased to offer clear and unambiguous choices on a question or questions of public policy.

- Substantially the entire adult population is guaranteed the right to vote.
- The rules for registering voters and for casting ballots are written and administered so that each eligible voter can readily cast one, and only one, ballot.
- No person is denied access to any information he or she wishes that is relevant to making his or her decisions on the issues.
- All persons or groups that wish to do so have full and fair opportunity to set forth their views of the issues, including access to the media of mass communications.
- Campaigns are conducted fairly in that neither law, violence, nor intimidation bars the advocates of any position from presenting their views or prevents the voters from learning those views.
- Votes are cast freely and secretly, and they are counted and reported accurately and honestly.

The foregoing standards add up to a model of democratic referendums; they do not constitute precise empirical descriptions of how referendums are actually conducted in every detail in any particular democracy. Rather, they define the criteria by which we can evaluate the quality of actual referendums conducted anywhere. Hence, when we evaluate referendums, whether in California or Switzerland or Micronesia, we are not dealing with mutually exclusive Aristotelean categories of democratic referendums that satisfy all the standards in every respect and with nondemocratic referendums that fall short of the standards in one or more respects. Rather we are dealing with referendums that are more or less democratic, depending on how closely their actual conduct approaches the model's standards.

That is how we shall approach our evaluation of the Micronesian plebiscites of 1983, applying each standard in turn.

Evaluation of the 1983 Micronesian Plebiscites

Phrasing of the Propositions. As we saw in chapter 2, the plebiscite in Palau began with a major controversy over the wording of the ballot's proposition 1–B on section 314 of the compact. There was a short-lived effort to rephrase the original proposition to emphasize the compact's restrictions on the power of the United States to store and transship nuclear materials in Palauan territory rather than to define the power itself. The original wording was restored by court order, however, and that wording seems to us to be neutral and fair. The FSM and the Marshall Islands profited from Palau's difficulties, and in neither of the later plebiscites was there any significant controversy—or reason for controversy—about the wording of the propositions.

In all three jurisdictions a second proposition asked the voter to choose between "independence" and some "other relationship with the United States" and then, if voters chose the latter, to write in the kind of other relationship they preferred. The open-ended nature of the second proposition put a considerable burden on the voters, most of whom had little experience or skills in writing about such matters.

The three sets of voters responded quite differently to the difficulties involved in part 2. Of all the persons voting, 75 percent voted on part 2 in the FSM, 56 percent in Palau, and 29 percent in the Marshall Islands. The proposition became moot in the FSM and the Marshalls when the compact was approved. In Palau, where the compact was declared defeated, the voters who voted on proposition 2 (56 percent of all voters) voted 56 percent for closer relations with the United States and 44 percent for independence. So far as we can tell, however, the votes on proposition 2 have not had a significant influence on subsequent negotiations, all of which have been directed at making changes so that the compact can win in a future plebiscite.

On balance, then, the final phrasings of the ballot propositions in all three jurisdictions appear to measure up well to our first standard.

Suffrage. The Micronesian plebiscites satisfied our second standard as well as any referendum anywhere. Every citizen who was eighteen years of age or older on the day of the plebiscite was entitled to vote, the other qualifications were minimal, and the suffrage was as wide as or wider than that in any democratic polity in the world.[3]

Registration and Voting. As we have noted, each of the three Micronesian jurisdictions had held numerous elections before 1983—elections for the Congress of Micronesia, for district legislatures, for municipalities, and for the members of the new constitutional governments. Moreover, there had been several advisory referendums in Palau and the Marshall Islands, a referendum in all three jurisdictions on the proposed constitution for a Micronesia-wide federation, and referendums in Palau and the Marshall Islands on their constitutions. At least one referendum in each jurisdiction had been observed and its conduct approved by observers sent by the Trusteeship Council of the United Nations. This history meant that all three jurisdictions had well-tested bodies of election laws and administrative procedures and corps of election administrators experienced in coping with the area's special problems.

In our judgment, each of the three jurisdictions faced several difficult and unusual problems and handled them well. One arose from the fact that for most Micronesians the holding of land rights in a particular locality is so important that they want to be registered to vote in that locality. Yet many Micronesians live and work in areas other than their own, some of them hundreds of miles away in other jurisdictions of Micronesia and some of them as far away as Hawaii and the mainland United States. The Micronesian authorities dealt with this problem by making it as easy as possible for voters to vote at locations other than where they were registered. One device was the familiar system of allowing voters to mark absentee ballots prior to election day, place them in sealed double envelopes with affidavits of eligibility, and mail them to the central counting place for inclusion with the ballots cast in the districts in which the absentee voters were registered. Another device, less familiar to Western observers but very useful in Micronesian conditions, was "in-person absentee voting," in which a voter registered in locality A presented himself or herself at the polling station in locality B, took an affidavit of eligibility, marked a ballot, and deposited it in a special box labeled for voters from locality A. The procedure was cumbersome: in most polling places, each affidavit was checked against a list of registered voters to make sure that the person applying was registered and had not already voted. In several places, notably Majuro and Ebeye in the Marshall Islands, there were too few election officials to handle the unexpectedly large number of voters using the procedure. The result in both places was a bottleneck at the registration table, long lines of voters awaiting their turns, and a need to keep the polls open hours after they were scheduled to close. So far as we could tell, however, hardly any voters grew discouraged and dropped out of line. Thus, despite its administrative difficulties, the new procedure did help to maximize the number of voters participating.

Another special problem arose from the high proportion of young and new voters in the electorate. In Micronesia 53 percent of the population is under the age of eighteen, compared with only 27 percent in the United States. This situation means that an unusually high proportion of the Micronesian population was coming of voting age near the time of the plebiscites, so there was a special need to make first-time registration as easy as possible. The FSM and the Marshall Islands met the need mainly by instituting election-day registration similar to the system used by four American states. By this procedure, unregistered but otherwise eligible voters could go to the polls on election day and make an affidavit that they were eligible to vote; their affidavits were then checked against such records as school and hospital records to verify the applicants' ages and residences.

108

There was no effective method of making sure that such persons had not already voted at some other locality, and this disturbed some observers. No charges of double voting were made, however, and we found no evidence of any instances of it. So it seems that the risk of fraud from election-day registration was minimal and that its benefits for young people and other first-time voters were considerable.

Perhaps the greatest problem of all was the logistical burden imposed by the scattering of small numbers of voters over great geographical distances. Palau and the Marshall Islands required that votes be cast locally but counted centrally. This requirement meant that ballots and instructions had to be delivered to the polling stations on all the islands and atolls before election day and that after the election the ballot boxes containing the marked and unmarked ballots had to be returned to Koror (Palau) and Majuro (the Marshalls) for counting. The transporting was not easy in either jurisdiction. There are about 600 kilometers of ocean between Koror and Tobi, Palau's most distant outer island, and 650 kilometers between Majuro and Rongelap in the Marshalls. Each of the Micronesian capitals has for some time been served by Air Micronesia, an affiliate of Continental Airlines, which operates relatively large Boeing 727 aircraft but visits Majuro, Kwajalein, Ponape, Truk, and Koror only three days a week westbound and three days eastbound. Moreover, only a few outer islands in both jurisdictions have airstrips of any kind, and the few available can accommodate only small aircraft. The others can be served only by boat. The three governments own and operate several relatively large ships for periodic field trips to take supplies to their outer islands, but such ships are expensive to operate (in many instances more than $1,000 per day) and only a limited number are available. There are plenty of smaller boats, but their utility depends upon relatively calm seas and good weather (in this the Micronesian governments were lucky: the weather just before and after all three plebiscites was moderate to good and did not delay boat traffic).

The FSM had the greatest problem of all: the state of Yap in the northwest corner lies 2,650 kilometers from Kosrae in the southeast corner, and transporting ballots to and from the outer islands to the capitals of the four states was especially expensive and time-consuming.

These logistical difficulties had several consequences. One was the considerable and unavoidable expense of getting the ballots to the outer islands—and for this reason alone the Micronesian plebiscites had considerably higher costs-per-vote-cast than are known to any Western country. Another consequence was the higher risk of ballot-box tampering: in many instances the ballot boxes on outer islands in both Palau and the FSM were not picked up and delivered to the central counting place until the following day, and this delay made them more vulnerable to stuffing, spoiling, and other kinds of fraud. Despite these apparent difficulties, however, few complaints were made and no instances of ballot-box tampering were proved. In Palau, some anticompact leaders complained that some ballots had been delivered in cardboard boxes rather than in official wooden ballot boxes; but the court held that no evidence of actual fraud had been produced, and AEI's scholars and the UN observers could find no such evidence. The logistical difficulties also prevented any official announcement of the results until several days after the balloting, but this delay seems to have been a problem only for impatient outside observers like ourselves.

Some Western observers were concerned that the great influence of the traditional chiefs on their followers might intimidate the voters from participating or expressing their true preferences. As we noted in chapter 3, there is strong evidence of such influence in parts of the Faichuk Islands in the FSM's state of Truk, where some traditional leaders tried to induce their followers to boycott the plebiscite altogether; but even there many people voted despite such pressures, and elsewhere there is no reason to believe that potential voters were frightened away from the polls. The influence of the traditional chiefs, as we suggest below, was manifested in other ways.

Some Western observers were also concerned that the ballots were not truly secret, especially in the FSM. In Palau and most places in the Marshall Islands, the on-island voters voted in crude but adequate plywood voting booths, but in the FSM it was common for voters to mark their ballots while seated in schoolroom desk chairs placed in the corner of the polling station (some even used the station's walls as writing surfaces). And in some areas of Majuro the Repmar government used, instead of polling booths, mobile polling stations—trucks carrying ballot boxes, polling officials, and policemen—which traveled along roads in rural areas, stopping to let voters cast their votes. In spite of these conditions, as we watched the votes being cast in Ponape, Truk, and Majuro we did not observe anyone trying to look over a voter's shoulder to see how he or she was voting. We concluded that Micronesians understand the importance of keeping the vote secret, and even the FSM's casual ballot-marking procedures did not appear to lead to any violation of that secrecy.

In the end, the turnout figures tell a great deal about how well the Micronesian plebiscites measured up to the standard of ease of registration and voting. As we have seen, the percentage of the voting-age population that voted was 88 percent in Palau, 63 percent in the FSM, and 83 percent in the Marshall Islands. These figures certainly compare very favorably with turnouts in most Western referendums. For example, in the state referendums in the United States in 1984 the average turnout was 49.6 percent, and the highest in any state was 62.5 percent (in Maine).[4] In Switzerland—to many the quintessence of Western democracy and certainly the world's greatest user of direct voting—the average turnout in referendums has been dropping steadily since the mid-1940s, and in the past ten years it has been just over 40 percent.[5] Accordingly we conclude that the Micronesian plebiscites satisfied the standards of fair voting and full popular eligibility and participation as well as most Western democracies and better than those that have made the heaviest use of referendums.

Voters' Access to Information. In the 1983 Micronesian plebiscites the voters could acquire information from three main sources: public information programs, public campaigns by the proponents and opponents, and private conversations with family, friends, and traditional leaders.

In all three jurisdictions, public information programs were organized by the Micronesian governments and funded by the United States. Each program began by translating the compact into the indigenous language or languages (one in the Marshall Islands, three in Palau, and eight in the FSM), printing copies of the versions in English and the indigenous languages, and distributing copies to the voters. As we have seen, this task was difficult, laborious, and expensive. In its English version, the compact is a long (well over two hundred single-spaced typewritten pages) and complicated document written in an opaque legalese. Moreover, the translations were probably less than perfectly faithful to the English original if only because the Micronesian languages often had no words or phrases exactly corresponding to the English-language legal concepts and niceties. To compound these difficulties, the documents were set before people who, as we have seen, are by tradition and custom more at home with oral than with written communications. Although we have no exact information, probably the printed versions of the compacts, prepared with such labor and expense, were read carefully by only a handful of citizens in each jurisdiction, and it is hard to avoid asking whether they were worth the great energy and expense. We believe that the answer is Yes, for several reasons. First, the printed compacts constituted universally available and last-resort references for determining just what the compact provided, and they were more authoritative than any oral summary or interpretation could be. Second, every Micronesian leader to whom we talked felt that the trans-

111

lations constituted vitally important evidence that the compact was a *Micronesian* as well as an American document; whether they were for or against the compact, most Micronesians would have been deeply offended if it had been available only in English. Third, in the course of making their line-by-line and concept-by-concept translations, the translators became knowledgeable about the compact's provisions, and many of them played valuable parts in the other initiatives of the voter-education programs.

Besides printing and distributing the translations, the public information programs took full account of Micronesians' preference for oral over written communications. First, the informants, many of whom were schoolteachers experienced in communicating complex materials, studied the compact's various provisions. Second, they traveled to just about every populated area in each jurisdiction and held public meetings at which they outlined the compact's provisions and answered questions about their meaning. Third, the public information programs prepared and presented several talks on radio (and a few on television) covering the same ground in much the same way; radio is by far the most important medium of mass communications everywhere in Micronesia. Thus all the citizens in each jurisdiction had many opportunities to learn about the compact in ways that were familiar and easy for them. Only a minority (estimates range from 20 percent to 35 percent of the electorate) attended the education programs' meetings, and a much larger number—although we have no way of estimating exactly how much larger—listened to some of the radio broadcasts. The point is that plenty of information was available to any Micronesian who wanted it, so the standard of public access to information was also well satisfied.

Several anticompact leaders, particularly in Palau and the Marshall Islands, charged that the education programs were inaccurate and biased and that they were really propaganda for Yes votes rather than neutral presentations of the facts. All that we could learn led us to agree with the judgment of the UN observers: in none of the three cases was there evidence of any deliberate effort by those who administered the public education programs to win Yes votes by giving inaccurate or misleading information, by overpraising the compact's benefits, or by concealing its costs. We agree with the UN's observers, however, that some anomalies inevitably arose because the three governments planning and conducting the public information programs each negotiated the compact's terms, thought the compact was a good deal, and hoped it would be approved. The only way around this circumstance probably would have been for an entirely neutral body, such as the UN, to fund and conduct the programs; but, so far as we could tell, no Micronesians ever requested such a procedure and, even if they had, it is highly unlikely that the UN would have assumed such a burden. Moreover, the anticompact forces had every chance to correct misinformation and make their cases against the compact. We conclude, then, that the UN observers were correct in their judgment that

> [while] there were some occasions [in Palau] when the dividing line between education and advocacy may have become a little blurred . . . the Mission . . . obtained no concrete evidence to substantiate charges that political education funds had been improperly used to influence voters.[6]

and that

> [In the Marshall Islands] care was taken to monitor the work of the teams and in particular to ensure that they did not advocate the acceptance of the compact. We were particularly impressed by the success of the task force members in retaining a very high degree of impartiality. Largely as a result of the work of the political education programme, the Marshallese were able to cast their votes with a knowledge of the major issues involved and with at least some idea of the alternative constitutional options.[7]

We would add that the education programs mounted by Brother Henry Schwalbenberg in the FSM and the Marshall Islands (see chapters 3 and 4) were important supplements to the official programs. His lectures, seminars, and written materials were complete, lucid, unbiased, and accurate. Moreover, unlike the official public information programs, Brother Henry's presentations were not confined solely to the contents of the compact; in addition, he provided *comparisons* between the compact and each of its alternatives on several matters of concern to the voters. He thus gave the Micronesians perhaps the clearest factual basis they had for choosing among the alternatives. His presentations together with those of the official education programs were as complete and as accurate a body of information available to the Micronesian voters as any produced for referendums in Western democracies.

Access to the Mass Media in the Public Campaigns. As we have seen, in the FSM there was almost no organized public opposition to the compact and almost nothing that could be called a public campaign on the issues beyond the voter-education program. Anyone who asked for free time on the government radio station to expound his or her views could get it on a first-come-first-served basis, but very few people made the request.

In Palau and the Marshall Islands, however, there were major organized opposition groups and considerable public campaigns on the issues. In both jurisdictions outside organizations and leaders—the antinuclear organizations in Palau and the MIATLP lawyers in the Marshalls—played major roles. They provided money, campaign materials, speakers, audiotapes and videotapes, and strategic advice to their Micronesian allies. Whatever their motives for intervening might have been, without doubt they greatly strengthened the local opposition's efforts and drew considerably more attention to the campaigns than would otherwise have been drawn. As allies of the local forces they had every right to participate, and our standards for democratic referendums require that opposition forces be given full access to the mass media to make their cases.

We believe that standard was fully met. In both jurisdictions a great deal of free time was made available on the government radio stations to anyone who wished to make presentations on the plebiscite's issues. In addition, the opposition organizations freely held public meetings and rallies, put up posters, and handed out campaign literature. In the Marshall Islands the opposition also published numerous full-page advertisements in the leading newspaper and handed out Western-style election souvenirs. Thus it is not surprising that we heard few complaints from opposition leaders in either Palau or the Marshall Islands that they were denied full and fair access to the mass communications media. Quite the contrary. In both places the compact's opponents made considerably more use of the mass media than its advocates did. But in the Micronesian cultures perhaps these are not the most important channels of political communication and influence.

The Role of the Traditional Chiefs. Perhaps the greatest departure from democratic ideals in the 1983 Micronesian plebiscites was the powerful role of the traditional chiefs. We have seen that in all three jurisdictions, but especially in the FSM and the Marshall Islands, many voters were more influenced by the private advice given them by their traditional chiefs than by the information and arguments set forth by the public information programs or by the public campaigns of the contending sides. We cannot say precisely how powerful the chiefs' influence was compared to other sources of influence, but most observers agree that it was a significant force both for and against the compact.

Several features of this influence disturb Western observers, including us. First, the voters subject to it do not make their choices as the autonomous individuals beloved of democratic theory; rather they, in effect, surrender their decision-making powers to their leaders. Second, there is a hint of coercion, direct or implied, that offends democratic ideals, although we cannot say precisely how much coercion was exerted.

This kind of influence is not, of course, unknown to Western polities: witness, for example, the political influence of landowners over tenants in pre-reform England and in France's *ancien regime,* or the hundreds of thousands of votes "delivered" by bosses and machines in most American big cities at least until World War II. But in the West these practices were and are generally condemned as undemocratic and corrupt, and over the years they have been widely attacked and often abolished. They still exist in a few places, but they have become the exception, not the rule. In any event, no democrat can ignore or welcome these practices in Micronesia no matter how deeply rooted they may be in the area's traditional cultures and ways of politics.

We repeat that we do not know exactly how powerful a role was played by the traditional chiefs, though we know their influence was a major force. We also know that in all three jurisdictions the chiefs were far from unanimous on the desirability of the compact. But our concern here is not with the direction of the chiefs' influence but with its pervasiveness and power. Of all the elements in the 1983 plebiscites, this, in our judgment, was the one that fell most short of the standards of democratic elections.

The generations of young Micronesians educated since the late 1940s in schools organized and funded by the United States have been educated primarily in Western values and behavior. Perhaps as they come of age and begin to take active roles in the Micronesian polities, as many already have, more and more will want to be their own persons politically and not merely the faithful followers of their traditional leaders. And perhaps more and more of the traditional chiefs themselves will become democratic leaders by putting their ideas and their leadership positions on the line in public elections. We take it as a good sign that some major chiefs, such as the Ibedul in Palau and Amata Kabua, an *iroij* in the Marshall Islands, are already doing so. Many aspects of traditional Micronesian cultures are precious and should be preserved, but we do not believe that the sub rosa political influence of the traditional chiefs is one of them.

Conclusion

All things considered, the Micronesian plebiscites of 1983 measured up very well indeed to most standards of democratic referendums. On most counts they were as well and fairly conducted as any in

Western democracies, and on some counts they were conducted better. This is no small achievement for third-world polities anywhere, but it is particularly remarkable for polities that must hold elections in the logistically and financially difficult circumstances facing Palau, the Federated States of Micronesia, and the Marshall Islands.

So we have little criticism and much praise to distribute. Some of the latter goes to the U.S. authorities, who by and large trusted the Micronesians to run their own elections. Some praise goes to the Micronesian public officials, elected and appointed, who drew up and administered the election rules. Some goes to the Micronesian partisans who organized the campaigns for and against the compact and conducted them with almost no violence or threats of violence. And some goes to the observers sent by the Trusteeship Council of the United Nations, who not only worked hard to observe what was going on but provided counsel and encouragement as well as legitimacy.

In the end, however, most of the credit for this considerable achievement in difficult circumstances goes to the Micronesian peoples. Of all the impressions we gathered in observing the plebiscites, the one that remains most vivid is the sight of the long lines of voters in Majuro and Ebeye standing patiently, many of them for five or six hours, in the high heat and humidity awaiting their turn to vote. Very few left before they had voted, they were uniformly cheerful and good-natured about the delay, and they seemed at least as dedicated to their civic duties as the average voters in, say, Berkeley, Bethesda, Vancouver, or Oxford. As one of our scholars stated in describing a voters' queue in the Marshall Islands:

> What was going on in the mind of a lady with a suckling baby who was collecting her ballot at midnight last Wednesday after queueing for six sweaty hours? It seems plain that she really cared about expressing, in all due formality, what she wanted for her country's future.[8]

And the UN observers added in the same vein:

> We shall all long remember the patient queues of people at Majuro and Kwajalein waiting sometimes for hours in the sun and sometimes late into the night to cast their votes. There could be no more eloquent testimony to the faith of such people in the democratic election process and their determination to play their part in it.[9]

Like other observers, we conclude that the peoples and leaders of the Micronesian polities are strongly committed to democratic values and procedures and are well prepared to assume their roles in a relationship of free association with the United States. The Micronesians have waited for more than four hundred years for such freedom, and we hope that they will soon pass the remaining barriers that stand in its way.

Notes

1. David Butler, Howard R. Penniman, and Austin Ranney, eds., *Democracy at the Polls: A Comparative Study of Competitive National Elections* (Washington, D.C.: American Enterprise Institute for Public Policy Research, 1981), p. 1.
2. We have distilled these standards from the vast literature on the meaning and requirements of democratic elections in general and referendums in particular. The items in that literature that we have found most useful include *Democracy at the Polls;* Giovanni Sartori, *Democratic Theory* (New York: Praeger Publishers, 1967); Joseph Schumpeter, *Capitalism, Socialism, and Democracy* (New York: Harper & Brothers, 1942); Carl J. Friedrich, *Constitutional Government and Democracy* (New York: Harper & Brothers, 1937); Robert A. Dahl, *A Preface to Democratic Theory* (Chicago: University of Chicago Press, 1956); David Butler and Austin Ranney, eds., *Referendums: A Comparative Study of Practice and Theory* (Washington, D.C.: American Enterprise Institute, 1978); Jean-Marie Denquin, *Référendum et plébiscite* (Paris: Librairie générale de droit et de jurisprudence, 1976); and Austin Ranney, ed., *The Referendum Device* (Washington, D.C.: American Enterprise Institute, 1981).
3. For the suffrage requirements in Western nations, see Ivor Crewe, "Electoral Participation," in *Democracy at the Polls*, table 10–1, pp. 220–23.
4. Austin Ranney, "Referendums and Initiatives, 1984," *Public Opinion* (December/January 1985), pp. 15–17.
5. For turnout rates in Switzerland and other Western democracies, see *Referendums*, chapter 3 and appendixes A and B.
6. *Report of the United Nations Visiting Mission to Observe the Plebiscite in Palau, Trust Territory of the Pacific Islands, February 1983* (UN Document T/1851, 1983), p. 35.
7. *Report of the United Nations Visiting Mission to Observe the Plebiscite in the Marshall Islands, Trust Territory of the Pacific Islands, September 1983* (UN Document T/1865, 1984), p. 14.
8. David Butler, "Democracy's Long Late Day on the Dots in the Ocean," *The Times* (London), September 14, 1983.
9. *Report of the United Nations Visiting Mission to Observe the Plebiscite in the Marshall Islands*, p. 15.

Index

(Page numbers in italics designate tables and figures.)

Abon, Laninruj, 80, 85
Absentee voting, 108
    See also Plebiscite in the FSM; Plebi-
    scite in the Marshall Islands; Plebi-
    scite in Palau
Ailinglaplap (Marshall Islands), 90, *98*
Ailuk (Marshall Islands), 79, *98*, 101
Aimeliik (Palau), 43, *44*, 46
Airai (Palau), 31, 43, *44*, 46
Air Micronesia, 109
Alab, 3
Allen, George, 80, 81
Allin Kein Ad, 89, 90
Alonz, Sylvester, 38
Amaraich, Andon, 53, 54, 58, 63, 64, 74
Andrike, Kinja, 80
Angaur (Palau), 43, *44*
Antinuclear groups, in Palau, 27, 29,
    33–38, 114
Armstrong, A. John, 5, 19
Arno (Marshall Islands), *98*
Aten, Erhart, 53
Aur (Marshall Islands), *98*
Australia, 33, 35

Babelthuap (Palau), 7, 24, 26, 36, 37
Ballots
    in democratic referendums, 105–106
    secrecy of, in plebiscites, 109–110
    two plebiscite questions on, 1
    See also Plebiscite in the FSM; Plebi-
    scite in the Marshall Islands; Plebi-
    scite in Palau
Balos, Ataji, 81, 88
Balos, Henchi, 81
Basilius, Bonifacio, 24, 31, 32
Beavers, John, 80
Bigler, Carmen, 80, 81, 84–86
Bikini (Marshall Islands), 79, 84, 91, *98*,
    100
Bilimon, Andrew, 80

de Brum, Oscar, 80, 86, 90, 101
Bryan, Tom, 53
Butler, David, 1

Cairns, Alan, 23–24
California, 9, 32
Campaign against Nuclear Power
    (CANP), 35
Carlos (Marshall Islands), 9
Caroline Islands, 1, 6
Chamorro (language), 7
Charter for the Congress of Micronesia,
    14, 15
Chutaro, Chuji, 89
Code of the Trust Territory, 15
COM. *See* Congress of Micronesia
Commonwealth Legislature (Northern
    Mariana Islands), 7
Commonwealth of the Northern Mariana
    Islands. *See* Northern Mariana Islands,
    Commonwealth of
Commonwealth status
    definition of, 62–63
    FSM, as alternative for, 17, 75
    Marshall Islands, as alternative for,
    17, 83, 85, 86, 89, 95, 97, *98–99*,
    101–102
    of Northern Mariana Islands, 7, 11,
    17, 93
    Palau, as alternative for, 17, 49
Community College of Micronesia, 59
Compact of Free Association
    negotiations for, 16–21
    traditional chiefs, influence of, 3–4,
    24
    U.S. rights and obligations under,
    18, 60–63
    See also Plebiscite in the FSM; Plebi-
    scite in the Marshall Islands; Plebi-
    scite in Palau; Traditional chiefs,
    influence of

election experience of, 94, 107
foreign rule of, 6, 90
form of government of, 3, 9–10, 12
geography of, 1, 9, 51
gross domestic product, 92
languages of, 9, 51, 82, 85, 111
and plebiscite (1977), 11, 94
and referendum (1978), 9, 12, 51, 94, 97
and referendum (1979), 9, 12, 89, 94, 97, 101
social structure of, 3
suits against United States, 79–80, 81–82, 83–84, 87, 89, 90–92, 100–101
traditional chiefs, influence of, 46, 89, 90, 100, 114–115
as a Trust Territory district, 11–12, 14
U.S. testing of nuclear devices in, 79–80
Voter Education Task Force, 85–86, 113
See also Economic aid, U.S.; Kwajalein Missile Range; Land rights; *Nitijela*; Plebiscite in Marshall Islands
Marshall Islands Atomic Testing Litigation Project (MIATLP), 79–80, 91
anticompact activities of, 84, 87–88, 89, 114
and results of plebiscite, 100–101, 102
Marshall Islands Journal, 80, 82, 87, 88, 89
Mason, Leonard, 81
McCoy, Janet J., 13, 54
Mejit (Marshall Islands), 79, *99*, 101
Melekeok (Palau), 43, *44*
Meller, Norman, 81
MIATLP. *See* Marshall Islands Atomic Testing Litigation Project
Micronesia (region)
demography of, 1, 108
economic dependence of, 2–3, 61
foreign rule of, 2, 5–6, 10, 52, 73, 90
geography of, 1, 6
nationalism, 6, 65
and plebiscite
difficulties of voting in, 107–111
public information programs, 111–113
as a strategic trust, 10–11
suffrage in, 107
traditional culture of, 2–3, 112, 115
See also Federated States of Micronesia; Marshall Islands, Republic of the; Northern Mariana Islands, Commonwealth of the; Palau, Republic of

Micronesia Seminar, 59–63, 64, 76
Micronesia Support Committee, 33–34
Mili (Marshall Islands), 89, *99*, 101
Missile-testing range. *See* Kwajalein Missile Range
Moen (FSM), 57, 58–59, 66, 68
Mogethin/What's Up? 59
Mokil (FSM), 73
Mortlock Islands (FSM), 57, 74
Moses, Resio, 54

Nakamura, Daiziro, 24, 38, 39
Nakamura, Mamoru, 24
Nakayama, Tosiwo, 15, 52, 66, 74–75
and plebiscite, 53, 55, 58, 64, 76
Namorik (Marshall Islands), *99*
Namu (Marshall Islands), *99*
Nang, Nag, 80
Nankens, 52, 64
Nanmwarkis, 52, 64
National Union, 59
Net (FSM), 65, *73*
New Guinea, 1
Newspapers, use of in plebiscites, 4
See also Plebiscite in the FSM; Plebiscite in the Marshall Islands; Plebiscite in Palau
Ngarchelong (Palau), 43, *44*
Ngardmau (Palau), 43, *44*, 46
Ngaremlengui (Palau), 43, *44*, 46
Ngatik (FSM), 73
Ngatpang (Palau), 43, *44*
Ngchesar (Palau), 43, *44*, 46
Ngeraard (Palau), 43, *44*, 46
Ngiwal (Palau), 43, *44*, 46
Niteak, Andrik, 81
Nitijela (Marshallese parliament), 3, 9–10, 11, 82, 94, 102
Northern Mariana Islands, Commonwealth of the, 1, 14
commonwealth status of, 11, 17, 93
Commonwealth Trial Court, 7
demography of, 7
form of government of, 7, 8
geography of, 6–7
languages of, 7
plebiscite (1975), 7, 17
Nuclear materials, U.S., 35
in FSM, storage and transshipment of, 20, 53, 60
in Marshall Islands, testing of, 17, 53, 79, 84
in Palau, storage and transshipment of, 1, 5, 23, 26, 28–29, 33–38, 106
See also Kwajalein Missile Range
Nukuoran (language), 9, 57, 58
Nukuoro (FSM), 73

123

"Voice of the Marshalls," 89, 93–94, 101

Wales, 1
Wolfinger, Richard
    and meetings with FSM officials, 53–54
    and meetings with Marshallese officials, 80–81
Wolian (language), 9, 57
World War I, 6
World War II, 6, 10, 53, 65, 115
Wotho (Marshall Islands), 79, 80, 81, 99, 101
Wotje (Marshall Islands), 79, 89, 99

Yaoch, S. J., Father Felix, 29
Yap (FSM), 5, 51, 52, 57, 69, 109
    legislature of, 14, 67, 77
    Palauan absentee voting in, 39, 45, 48
    and plebiscite observers, 53–54
    population of, 9
    results of plebiscite in, 71, 72, 75
    television, campaign use of, 58, 59
    as a Trust Territory district, 8, 11–12
    voter turnout in, 70, 71
Yapese (language), 9, 57
Yoma, Strik, 57

Zeder, Fred, 37, 54, 82

A Note On The Book

This book was edited by
Ellen Dykes and Janet Schilling of the
Publications Staff of the American Enterprise Institute.
The index was prepared by Margaret Benjaminson.
Pat Taylor designed the cover,
using a photograph taken by Howard Penniman.
The maps were drawn by Hördur Karlsson.
The text was set in Palatino, a typeface designed by Hermann Zapf.
Coghill Book Typesetting Company, of Richmond, Virginia,
set the type, and Thomson-Shore, Inc.
of Dexter, Michigan, printed and bound the book,
using permanent, acid-free paper made by the S.D. Warren Company.

SELECTED AEI PUBLICATIONS

The American Elections of 1982, Thomas E. Mann and Norman J. Ornstein, eds., (1983, 203 pp., cloth $16.95, paper $8.95)

Australia at the Polls: The National Elections of 1980 and 1983, Howard R. Penniman, ed. (1983, 351 pp., $14.95)

Ethnocentrism in Foreign Policy: Can We Understand the Third World? Howard J. Wiarda (1985, 67 pp., $3.95)

How Does the Constitution Secure Rights? Robert A. Goldwin and William A. Schambra, eds. (1985, 125 pp., cloth $13.95, paper $5.95)

Democracy at the Polls: A Comparative Study of Competitive National Elections, David Butler, Howard R. Penniman, and Austin Ranney, eds. (1981, 367 pp., cloth $16.25, paper $8.25)

Switzerland at the Polls: The National Elections of 1979, Howard R. Penniman, ed. (1983, 198 pp., cloth $16.95, paper $8.95)

• *Mail orders for publications to:* AMERICAN ENTERPRISE INSTITUTE, 1150 Seventeenth Street, N.W., Washington, D.C. 20036 • *For postage and handling, add 10 percent of total; minimum charge $2, maximum $10 (no charge on prepaid orders)* • *For information on orders, or to expedite service, call toll free 800-424-2873 (in Washington, D.C., 202-862-5869)* • *Prices subject to change without notice.* • *Payable in U.S. currency through U.S. banks only*

AEI ASSOCIATES PROGRAM

The American Enterprise Institute invites your participation in the competition of ideas through its AEI Associates Program. This program has two objectives: (1) to extend public familiarity with contemporary issues; and (2) to increase research on these issues and disseminate the results to policy makers, the academic community, journalists, and others who help shape public policies. The areas studied by AEI include Economic Policy, Education Policy, Energy Policy, Fiscal Policy, Government Regulation, Health Policy, International Programs, Legal Policy, National Defense Studies, Political and Social Processes, and Religion, Philosophy, and Public Policy. For the $49 annual fee, Associates receive
- a subscription to *Memorandum,* the newsletter on all AEI activities
- the AEI publications catalog and all supplements
- a 30 percent discount on all AEI books
- a 40 percent discount for certain seminars on key issues
- subscriptions to any two of the following publications: *Public Opinion,* a bimonthly magazine exploring trends and implications of public opinion on social and public policy questions; *Regulation,* a bimonthly journal examining all aspects of government regulation of society; and *AEI Economist,* a monthly newsletter analyzing current economic issues and evaluating future trends (or for all three publications, send an additional $12).

Call 202/862-6446 or write: AMERICAN ENTERPRISE INSTITUTE
1150 Seventeenth Street, N.W., Suite 301, Washington, D.C. 20036